Does the Law Morally Bind the Poor?

or

What Good's the Constitution When You Can't Afford a Loaf of Bread?

Critical America

General Editors: RICHARD DELGADO and JEAN STEFANCIC

Does the Law Morally Bind the Poor?

or

What Good's the Constitution When You Can't Afford a Loaf of Bread?

R. George Wright

NEW YORK UNIVERSITY PRESS
New York and London

NEW YORK UNIVERSITY PRESS
New York and London

Copyright © 1996 New York University

Grateful acknowledgment is made to the Catholic University Law Review for permission to publish a revised version of my article "The Progressive Logic of Criminal Responsibility and the Circumstances of the Most Deprived," 43 Cath. U.L. Rev. 459–504(1994).

Library of Congress Cataloging-in-Publication Data

Wright, R. George.
Does the law morally bind the poor, or, What good's the
Constitution when you can't afford a loaf of bread? / R. George Wright.
p. cm. — (Critical America)
Includes bibliographical references and index.
ISBN 0-8147-9294-4 (cloth: acid-free paper)
1. Criminal liability—United States. 2. Public welfare—Law and legislation—United States. 3. Poor—Civil rights—United States.
I. Title. II. Series.
KF9243.5.W75 1996   95-50202
345.73'04—dc20   CIP
[347.3054]

New York University Press books are printed on acid-free paper, and their binding materials are chosen for strength and durability.

Manufactured in the United States of America

10 9 8 7 6 5 4 3 2 1

For Mary,

with thanks to
Karon Bowdre
Richard Delgado
Joshua Dressler
Lori Hackleman
Judy McAlister
Jeffrie G. Murphy
Trisha Olson
Niko Pfund
Jean Stefancic
Kimberly Schooley

contents

What are the pros and cons of living in a broken trash compactor? The advantages are actually many and substantial. The danger of electrocution, for example, is less than that of sleeping near a 600-volt electrified train rail. The chances of being hit by a stray bullet are less than in some housing projects. Of course, one must not too quickly generalize about such matters. A housing project resident might reduce the risk of unintended gunshot wounds by such expedients as sleeping in the bathtub.

We should not overlook some of the less obvious advantages of the broken trash compactor lifestyle. Any food discarded into the compactor offers a win-win proposition. Either the discarded food is actively decomposing, or it is not. If it is not decomposing, it is in some sense edible. If, on the other hand, it is decomposing, other advantages exist. For one, decomposing food provides more cushioned bedding material than, say, a porcelain bathtub. More important, the chemical decomposition of rotting food generates heat. Just this sort of chemical reaction may mean the difference between freezing to death and not.

Other advantages of the trash compactor lifestyle, such as its excellent protection against windchill, if not against vermin, are obvious, and need no further rehearsal. Instead, let us note one significant disadvantage not yet factored into our calculus. We have carefully specified the trash compactor to be broken. But what if it does not stay broken? What if, one day, it is repaired and restored to active service? What if this takes place without advance public notice or, in particular, notification of the trash compactor's resident? What, finally, if the inhabitant of the trash compactor is, every night, at least dimly aware of just this possibility?

The actual playing out of this macabre scenario is extremely uncommon, though apparently not entirely unheard of.[1] It is worth note not for the frequency of its occurrence, but for its unusually stark metaphorical import. Perhaps in the absence of any official malice at any stage, a living human being is unconsentingly merged into crushed societal refuse.

It is difficult to identify with those whose lives focus centrally on broken trash compactors. Human compactification is, for us, cartoonlike or, at worst, the fate of minor characters in James Bond movies. It is hardly the stuff of nightmares, or of familiar personal decision making. But nonconsensual compactification and disposal is merely an extreme example of a much broader range of incidents, circumstances, and lifestyles most of us have difficulty fathoming.

What, for example, would we think if in the course of our daily lives, we noticed that the cords ordinarily used to adjust a set of window sashes were no longer there? A number of possibilities might occur to us. Most of us, however, would not immediately consider that intravenous drug users had taken the cords for the purpose of constricting their blood circulation.

For some, however, this possibility would be quite real. Such persons, it is fair to say, live in a world different from ours. This book seeks to trace out a few of the most basic legal and political implications of life in circumstances far bleaker than those with which most of us are familiar.

The poor live in the same world as the rest of us, yet their world is crucially different. This is both a paradox and a commonplace. The public mishandling of this paradoxical commonplace frequently injures the poor.

The better-off tend to project their own categories and experiences onto the poor. This is not a mysterious process. Even at our best-intentioned, we have limited capacities for empathy and imagination. And from the standpoint of the most deprived persons, the problem of communication becomes a paradox. A person who lived all her life under circumstances of severe deprivation, yet was able to accurately convey what it is like to live a life of chronic, severe deprivation, would be a walking impossibility. Chronic, severe deprivation inevitably impairs the capacity to communicate what such a form of life is like.

Of course, the gulf between even the most desperately poor and the better-off is not utterly unbridgeable. Hunger, cold, and perceived contempt are very widely disvalued. The well-off can imagine that it would be somehow unappealing to be homeless, to be regarded contemptuously, or to be routinely hungry. The poor are certainly capable of articulating these truths of experience.

But there remain limits beyond which the categories and experiences of the better-off should not be extended. Frequently, the law does not respect these limits. Federal sentencing law provides an example.

The law generally refuses to consider the creed or religious affiliation of the criminal defendant in imposing sentence. In doing so, the law obviously draws on basic elements in the liberal egalitarian tradition. But federal sentencing law then goes on, in the name of impartiality and neutrality, to treat privilege and privation in the same way.

In effect, federal sentencing law says that just as it would be unfair to sentence defendants differently on the basis of their atheism or Episcopalianism, so it would be unfair to consider the convicted defendant's life of privilege or of grimly unrelieved severe economic deprivation. Just as the inside trader is not sentenced more harshly because of a privileged economic background, so the crack buyer is not punished less severely in light of her less privileged circumstances.

Criminal sentencing occurs, however, only at a late stage in the judicial process. The law fails to take proper account of the circumstances of the severely deprived in more basic respects. Most of us, for example, consider ourselves somehow morally bound by the Constitution and its basic political institutions and processes. We tend to assume that even the most chronically, abjectly poor are similarly morally bound. Most of us further assume that we normally bear full moral responsibility for our criminal acts. We tire of the range and variety of excuses offered for criminal behavior, and we reinforce our basic assumption of individual responsibility. Ordinarily, we extend this assumption to cover even the most severely deprived persons. Finally, we commonly assume that whatever may be the limits of legally recognized defenses to otherwise criminal acts, the same limits should generally apply to all persons, including the most economically desperate. Thus we typically reject what has been called the economic necessity defense.

This book argues that each of these extensions of experience from the well off to the most severely deprived violates logic and fairness. The substance of the arguments will unfold below. For now, it is useful merely to note that the arguments in each of the above contexts are logically independent. One may reject the conclusion that the chronically poorest are, precisely by virtue of their deprivation, not morally bound by our present constitutional system. But even if one does so, it is still possible to conclude that the chronically poorest, or some portion thereof, frequently do not bear the moral responsibility for their acts that the criminal justice system maintains they do. This conclusion, too, may be rejected. But in turn, it is then still possible to conclude that even if the most severely deprived bear full moral responsibility, legal defenses such as necessity should logically excuse some otherwise criminal acts committed under desperate economic circumstances.

Each of these admittedly unpopular conclusions is, consecutively, argued for below. While the conclusions are unpopular, the premises of each argument are intended to be broadly acceptable. There is little point in not beginning the arguments on widely shared ground. The conclusions would be of little interest if they were reached only from spectacularly controversial premises. The reader is merely cautioned that the arguments must be confronted separately. To refute one is not necessarily to refute the others. On the other hand, accepting any of the separate arguments below tends to justify, if not promote, significant legal and social change.

We cannot say with any precision how many persons actually fall within the scope of the populations discussed below. The numbers concerned will in fact vary. Chapter 1, on legal obligation, refers broadly to the chronically poor. Chapter 2, on criminal moral responsibility, refers to the most deprived persons. Chapter 3, on the necessity defense, refers more concretely to groups such as the involuntarily homeless. But estimates of the number of homeless persons vary quite substantially, and Chapter 3 attempts no census. In each chapter, the discussion refers to a substantial number of persons living under rather grim circumstances, persons with important moral claims on our attention.

Grimness is in this sense largely a matter of economics. But let us stipulate that living under grim circumstances, in chronic poverty, or being severely deprived is not exclusively a matter of economics. Other categories, including race and gender, have a role to play as well. Some persons who are homeless, for example, may face racial discrimination while others do not. Severe deprivation is hardly spread evenly across demographic categories, and we can hardly understand fully anyone's deprivation unless we account for her group affiliations. In the main, however, the arguments below seek to establish broad but quite significant conclusions, without thoroughly exploring the differences among those who are most severely deprived. This is an important task, but it is not our present task.

Let us turn then to the logically basic question of the relationship between poverty and constitutional obligation.

Does the Constitution

Morally Bind the Poor?

chapter one

This chapter explores a crucial, but largely undiscussed, problem in American constitutional jurisprudence. The problem is not difficult to state: Many Americans live through remarkable deprivation and disadvantage. Their stories differ widely, but common elements include inadequate nutrition, desperate poverty, sheer physical danger, or even homelessness. It is nevertheless widely assumed that such persons are morally obligated, or generally morally bound, by the United States Constitution. Much of the Constitution does not impose direct duties of compliance on ordinary citizens. But it is still assumed that the poor, along with others, must work within the established constitutional framework. Further, they must accept, as authorized and legitimate, actions undertaken in carrying out constitutional provisions. But it is not clear why this should be so. This chapter critically examines the arguments for holding those we may call the abject poor to be morally bound by the Constitution. Those lines of argument turn out to be unsatisfactory, for reasons that are unique to the circumstances of the abject poor. The chapter concludes by briefly reflecting on the moral limits that may still legitimately bind those persons not genuinely morally bound by the Constitution.

In the American constitutional tradition, the most natural explanation of why the abject poor, or indeed anyone else, should be held bound by the Constitution relies on consent or social contract. The courts have commonly referred to at least some such understanding, and the framers are commonly thought to have done so as well. The idea of a social contract has been interpreted in a number of ways. Our focus, however, is simply on the presence or absence of some form of voluntary consent in determining whether persons should be held morally obligated to obey a particular government. Social contract theory holds that only by intentional and voluntary consent signaled to another can a free and autonomous person come to be obligated to obey. Even if consent is not by itself sufficient to create a morally binding obligation, consent is at least a necessary condition for such an obligation to exist.

It is plainly possible to launch broad attacks against any form of a social contract or consent theory of obligation. Classic as well as contemporary versions of such broad-based attacks are well known. Our purpose, however, is not to add to or respond to this literature. We will instead assume that all the theories of obligation we discuss in this chapter are coherent and can be sensibly applied in some cases. Thus our initial focus is on whether consent theory can establish a moral obligation specifically on the part of the chronically abject poor to adhere to the American Constitution, including its amendment process, along with the moral implications for such persons if consent theory fails in this regard. While the Constitution does not, for the most part, command abjectly poor people to obey or to do particular things, the Constitution does claim to establish a uniquely authorized, legitimately binding framework that the poor and others are to recognize and work within.

Whether the abject poor are thus rightly bound by the Constitution may depend on the substantive provisions of the Constitution, the process of proposing, negotiating, and ratifying the Constitution, or some combination of the two. We must therefore consider both the substance of the Constitution and the procedures associated with its adoption when we consider the ways in which persons might be said to consent.

We may begin by thinking about the Constitution in a general way. It is often observed that the Constitution is largely, if not exclusively, a guarantor of what are referred to as "negative," as opposed to "positive," liberties or rights. Of course, the Constitution does far more than recognize or protect rights and liberties. But we may, for our purposes, safely focus on the Constitution insofar as it speaks, or fails to speak, to such rights and liberties. The differences between negative and positive liberties and between negative and positive rights are actually quite murky, but rough distinctions may be attempted.

Let us begin with a few examples. Rights to education, housing, or welfare, whether actually recognized or merely proposed, and whether they are legal rights or moral rights, are commonly thought of as positive rights. In contrast, a right to not be deprived, via false imprisonment by the government, of one's liberty without due process would be a negative right. To not be defrauded or assaulted by some private actor would also typically be thought of as negative rights.

These examples suggest that at least in some cases, positive rights tend to be more publicly expensive or more difficult to fulfill than negative rights. In addition, given some arbitrary historical baseline or some assumed status quo, positive rights may redistribute wealth more than negative rights. Positive rights may seem to require more affirmative or active government intervention than do negative rights, at least from the perspective of the chosen historical baseline.

Bringing these strands together, we might argue that a private party may respect the negative right of every person to not be directly assaulted by that particular party merely by doing nothing at all, or by doing anything other than engaging in an assault. On the other hand, it may be difficult for a private party, or even a government, to so inexpensively or so passively fulfill, universally or even for a single person, a positive right to welfare. Most of us can refrain from assaulting more people than we can readily afford to feed. Not assaulting one person rarely makes it more difficult to not assault another person, whereas feeding one person may, in more cases, diminish the resources by which we might also feed another person.

This gives us some idea of the distinction between negative and positive rights. The distinction, on the other hand, between negative and positive liberties is rarely formulated in the same way twice, but we can at least bring out some of the recurring themes. In the sense in which we are most interested, negative liberty means something like the absence of socially imposed restraints on the range or value of one's choices and actions. Positive liberty, on the other hand, means liberty to obtain what one wants or what is really in one's interests, generally through the affirmative assistance and support of other people. Positive liberty is often associated with some conception of self-realization, self-development, growth, or even rationality itself. Again, the distinction between negative and positive liberty may be suspect, but we may for our purposes think of positive liberty as the actual attainment by some party of some desirable state of affairs.

Using these distinctions, we may ask about the nature of the federal Constitution and its substantive rights provisions. Often, the

Constitution is associated with negative rights or liberties. But the Constitution cannot be categorized as purely "negative," along these dimensions, in any simple and exceptionless way. If we look to admittedly recent, but apparently stable, Supreme Court interpretations of basic constitutional rights, we can recognize at least a few "positive" elements.

For example, in *Gideon v. Wainwright* the Court interpreted the Sixth Amendment, via the due process clause of the Fourteenth Amendment, to require the states to provide legal counsel for at least some indigent criminal defendants requesting such assistance. Thus not all due process claims involve only clearly negative rights. Under *Gideon*, the indigent criminal defendant has an enforceable legal claim to services the market value of which might far exceed the defendant's net wealth. Substantial wealth redistribution may thus occur. This right is of direct, immediate value only to criminal defendants, and is not readily transferrable or convertible into other sorts of rights or values. But this does not mean that the right is not "positive" in character. The right takes the form not merely of government noninterference in the indigent defendant's likely futile attempt to hire private counsel, but of affirmative government provision of a valuable, otherwise unaffordable service. One might also say that indigent persons, whether charged with a crime or not, may have some sort of a right to police protection from private criminal acts. This right, too, might well be redistributive, or of a value beyond the indigent's ability to pay. But such a right is, currently, not of constitutional dimension, and is certainly not legally enforceable in any specific way, as a right to appointed counsel might be.

Even the classically "negative" right to freedom of speech may have at least some minimal, if difficult to specify, positive or affirmatively redistributive elements under the case law. It may well be that the Constitution, in at least some cases, requires the government to foot the bill, in the form of increased costs of police protection, insurance, or merely increased maintenance and sanitation costs, for parades or rallies. It may thus be that the free speech clause sometimes prevents the government from requiring the organizer or speaker to either fully internalize these costs or refrain from speaking. It is at least unclear, for example, that a government could require an organization of poor persons to demonstrate its financial ability to pay the reasonable additional costs of, say, state employees' picking up discarded leaflets.

These examples certainly do not exhaust the range of federal constitutional rights in which the government assumes an affirmative, at least modestly redistributive role. But as we have seen, the general tenor and character of the rights protected by the Constitution is indeed largely "negative." The positive rights protected by the Constitution are few in number and of less than vital practical significance for most of the abject poor.

This is not to suggest that, for example, their currently recognized positive constitutional right to a waiver of a divorce filing fee must be regarded by all abjectly poor persons as trivial. But such a positive constitutional right must pale into insignificance in comparison with many of the potential positive constitutional rights currently denied by the Court. This is also not to suggest that the abject poor all share common histories, ideologies, priorities, or even circumstances beyond some level of detail. But on any view of reasonable choice, most chronically abjectly poor persons will recognize their interest in access to food, shelter, education, physical safety, or employment as more vital than most of the currently recognized positive constitutional rights. And it is precisely those most basic interests in food, shelter, education, physical safety, and employment that our society leaves contingent, substantially uncertain in practice, and unprotected by our federal Constitution.

To be sure, some individual states recognize some sort of state constitutional right to an education, but this is neither universally meaningful among the states nor guaranteed at the federal constitutional level. The idea of any sort of federal constitutional right to employment has not even been taken seriously, nor has a general right to even minimal government efforts to provide for some degree of sheer physical safety or security from private assault. This is, upon reflection, an extremely odd and striking state of affairs, even given classical liberal distrust of government. Such rights are, in one way or another, strongly emphasized in liberal and social contract theorists as diverse as Hobbes, Spinoza, Harrington, Locke, Hume, and Condorcet.

These vital interests are, at least for the abject poor, often not only not constitutionally or otherwise legally guaranteed, but quite likely unfulfilled by any means in practice. The absence of a constitutional right would be arguably inconsequential if, in practice, one's private efforts, the market, other sorts of law, or private charity almost invariably provided what the Constitution had failed to guarantee. But this is, in varying degrees, simply not the case for the most vital interests of the abject poor. Can we say, for example, that even in the absence of any constitutional protection for physical safety, the poor and homeless really need not worry about their own physical safety?

In addition, there is no reasonable certainty that any, let alone all, of the most vital interests of the abject poor will eventually be constitutionally recognized, at least within the next generation or so. While such recognition is possible, it would be plainly imprudent for the abject poor to assume that it is likely. It would thus be imprudent for many of the abject poor to endorse the present Constitution on the grounds that it will, over the reasonably near term, likely be transformed to accommodate their most basic needs and interests. It is, of course, possible to assume that the abject poor care only about events that will be occurring decades from now, but that unrealistic assumption would serve only to rob social contract theory of most of its interest.

We are left with a Constitution featuring only few and generally less than practically crucial positive rights and liberties, and no strong likelihood of this changing dramatically in the near future. Let us then consider how this state of affairs fits with a social contract or consent theory of why the chronically abject poor should be held morally bound to obey or work within the established constitutional framework.

There are two important general lines of consent-based argument. According to the first line of argument, the substance and content of the Constitution are such that the abject poor ought reasonably to consent to its terms, whether they actually consent or not. The second line of argument holds that the abject poor have in fact consented or agreed to the Constitution, expressly or tacitly, in circumstances under which that consent may rightly be held morally binding.

We may consider the first possible line of argument to involve merely the hypothetical consent of the abject poor, in that the argument aims not at showing any actual consent, but at showing that insofar as the abject poor are reasonable, they, perhaps along with the nonpoor, would freely consent to the Constitution if presented with the choice.

Let us take the chronically abject poor as they are, and as knowing themselves to be chronically, abjectly poor. Concretely, we may think of them as chronically, abjectly poor precisely because their relationship to basic sustenance, shelter, education, physical safety, and employment is known to them to be substantially uncertain, unreliable, or subject to disruption for personally uncontrollable reasons. Of course, not all such persons may care about all these dimensions of life. The very elderly, for example, may have only a limited direct interest in practical access to a safe primary education. We shall, however, treat this as a noncrucial complication.

If the poor know their own general circumstances, along with some basic facts about our economy and society, including the availability of great collective wealth and discretionary income, and the practical possibilities for redistributing wealth at some possible cost in inefficiency and disincentives, they reasonably must ask how the current Constitution promotes their basic interests and values by comparison with other possible constitutional regimes. They will reasonably ask whether a different feasible mixture of negative and positive constitutional rights might, from the standpoint of their basic interests and values, be significantly preferable.

We are assuming that the abject poor, along with everyone else, will be thinking partly in terms of rights and claims of right. This is perhaps a controversial assumption, as the proper role of rights claims is itself controversial. Talking in terms of rights is sometimes thought to lend itself to excessive individualism, selfishness, absolutism, or evasion of responsibility and lack of civic-mindedness. We will nevertheless assume some degree of rights talk, and that any constitution consensually arrived at will incorporate some sorts of rights protection. Our task, after all, is to determine whether our current Constitution could reasonably be consented to by the poor, or otherwise morally bind the poor. Avoiding rights talk is no less controversial than relying on rights talk, and avoiding a rights analysis may actually bias the inquiry against any moral obligation to our current rights-laden Constitution. If talk of rights should be avoided, we can, admittedly, hardly condemn the Constitution for not protecting the rights of the poor. But on the other hand, why should the poor reasonably endorse our current Constitution if, by assumption, that Constitution is misguided insofar as it focuses on any sorts of rights?

We have also assumed that the poor, along with everyone else, will decide whether to consent to the Constitution based largely on their own most crucial interests, individually or collectively, over some reasonable time frame, perhaps in conjunction with other basic values. It is difficult to see how some such assumption could be avoided by a consent theory. We could instead assume that the poor strongly identify with the interests of the rich, but this would not be of much interest for our purposes unless we also assumed that the rich strongly identified with the interests of the poor. We will instead assume only limited cross-class interest.

Now, we can imagine some poor persons who do not mind starving or being homeless, on the theory that such starvation or homelessness makes it possible and likely that their children or other family members will be quite well-off financially. We may fairly assume, however, that many poor people will detect no such iron linkage between the remarkably severe impoverishment of some and otherwise unattainable well-being for the families of those thus severely impoverished.

These assumptions are not meant to restrict the sorts of considerations to which the poor may wish to attend. It is commonly thought that rights are often based on some idea of interests. But the poor may equally look to basic needs, which may of course overlap with interests, or to dignitary values. We do not wish to insist that the reasonableness of the poor take any special form.

The question then becomes whether the abject poor, perhaps along with others, should reasonably consent to our present Constitution or something essentially similar. They would presumably look generally to compatibility with their basic interests, needs, and values under alternative constitutional regimes, in practice, over time.

Some theorists may assume that even the poorest should sacrifice possible gains under some possible constitutions in order to minimize the risk of someday occupying the most horrifying social roles. We need not assume that the poor will seek to avoid as much risk as possible. On the other hand, if the poor are asked to consent without knowing whether they will be rich or poor, prudence would dictate that they avoid authorizing a regime in which one might well be chronically unemployed or even homeless. Guarding against the possibility of extreme poverty hardly requires that typical persons live under near-poverty conditions. Thus it seems unlikely that the homeless would consent to a regime involving significant involuntary homelessness even if they did not know who would turn out to be homeless. There is also no reason to assume masochistic self-denial on the part of the poor. Nor would it be reasonable on the part of the poor to assume that no constitutional regime can improve or worsen what would otherwise be their lot in life. Whether the chosen constitution permits slavery, for example, makes a difference.

When the abject poor consider our current Constitution, they will see a document that generally protects negative rights, along with a limited number of generally less than vital positive rights. They should recognize that there is no clear reason to believe that this will dramatically change anytime soon. But for the abject poor, the difference between negative and positive rights is often crucial in practice: given some chosen baseline, positive rights generally require more affirmative government assistance, redistribution, and provision than negative rights.

For these reasons, alleged rights to minimal subsistence, minimal housing, education, some degree of physical safety, or employment are normally thought of as positive rights. An alleged right to minimal subsistence may, along with the other potential positive rights, vary greatly in its scope and stringency. But if such a right is to be useful and valuable for the most poor, it must extend beyond a negative right to be free of direct state interference in one's lawful attempts to earn one's bread. Similarly, an alleged right to some degree of physical safety might be conceived of in many ways. But if the aim or underlying interest is as we would suppose it to be, the right to physical safety must extend beyond the merely negative right against government interference with lawful self-defense, and beyond the largely negative rights to due process and freedom from cruel and unusual punishment or other governmental threats to safety. Most reasonable poor persons object to being beaten in the streets not only by police, but by purely private persons as well.

The poor are likely to reason that there is something seriously incomplete in a right not to be inappropriately shot by government actors if the government could, but is not required, to do significantly more to reduce the danger of more private threats to one's life. Nor is it fully satisfactory to enjoy a right not to be subject to racial discrimination in hiring if substantial, socially alterable barriers of other sorts to meaningful employment remain. In such cases, the reasons underlying the negative right largely, if not entirely, extend to one or more positive rights as well, whether or not the positive rights will be in any sense more socially costly than the negative rights. Those who take the negative right seriously tend logically to take at least some related positive right seriously as well.

This is not to deny that the poor will appreciate any number of structural and individual rights provisions of the current Constitution. But neither should we deny that there is a set of alternative constitutions, with different mixtures of different sorts of negative and positive rights, to which the poor would more reasonably adhere. We need not argue that most or all of the poor would insist on some version of all the various positive rights referred to above. And we need not argue that there is some particular constitution that would be the first choice of all reasonable abject poor, or even upon which all reasonable abject poor would eventually settle. The crucial point is simply that the chronically abject poor, under the circumstances we have specified, would reasonably tend to prefer some apparently practically viable constitution substantially different from and more "positive" than our current Constitution.

We shall elaborate on this argument a bit further below. But let us first conclude our general inventory of the broad kinds of relevant social contract theory by turning from hypothetical or reasonable consent theories to theories of actual consent. Specifically, we must ask whether contemporary poor persons have, in general, in some fashion actually given a morally binding consent to the current Constitution.

Here again, we might answer in the negative by citing any of the broad objections to or limitations on "actual consent" versions of social contract theory. But again, it is not our intention to endorse or reject such a broad approach. We will assume that actual consent theory is, as a general matter, perfectly viable. Instead, we are concerned with applying actual consent theory to the special circumstances of the abject poor.

To determine the validity of consent by the poorest persons, we must consider voluntariness, coercion, and freedom, starting points or presumed baselines, personal capacities, and resource endowments; we must consider bargaining power and fairness in bargaining.

Some of the relevant issues are subtle. Others are not. It is difficult to argue, for example, that the contemporary poor have actually consented to the Constitution based somehow on the claim that the poor actually consented at the time of the drafting and ratification of the Constitution. Plainly, the closest counterparts of today's abject poor were, at the time of the adoption of the Constitution, typically disenfranchised at every stage of the drafting and ratification process. Given the clear historical record, it may be less implausible to find actual consent by today's abject poor independently of any supposed actual consent on the part of the poorest some two hundred years ago.

Merely for the sake of advancing the argument, we may boldly stipulate that most of today's poor have actually made some sign, or failed to disavow some sign, that is thought by most persons to indicate actual consent to the Constitution. Even this heroic assumption, however, cannot establish valid consent. This is because in the case of the abject poor, the logical prerequisites to being morally bound by purported acts of consent are typically still not met. To see this, let us match up what is logically required for morally binding actual consent against the circumstances of the abject poor.

In most formulations, social contract theory requires individual consent by rational, free, and equal persons. Of course, problems arise when we ask what kinds and degrees of departure from perfect rationality, knowledge, freedom, or equality are permissible. It seems reasonable to suspect that such problems loom large in the case of the chronically abject poor.

Let us consider first the near truism that the kinds of rights that are recognized, their distribution, and the degree of their enforcement reflect how wealth and power, including education, are distributed in a society. Plainly, the abject poor lack power, privilege, and wealth relative to their fellow social contractors. The gross disparities between the abject poor and the middle class along these dimensions call into serious question the validity or moral bindingness of any purported act of consent by the abject poor.

Neither the poor nor anyone else can be voted into genuinely consenting by the majority of a society. This requirement of individual consent is naturally associated with the idea that a valid social contract fairly advances the interests of all those obligated thereby. At a minimum, if the interests of all those to be held bound are to be fairly advanced, the terms of the social contract, or of the constitution itself, cannot disproportionately reflect the interests of those able to influence those terms through their greater financial resources. Similarly, the terms of the social contract or constitution cannot unduly reflect the brute social fact that the interests of the better-off would be only mildly threatened by any refusal of the abject poor to consent.

Thus, even if the abject poor could be said to have made some sign of purported consent to the Constitution, they could not be held morally bound by that act if the substantive terms of the

Constitution or the bargaining process leading up to the purported sign of consent are themselves morally questionable.

We have already noted the general absence from the Constitution of the sorts of positive rights that would apparently promote the most basic interests of the abject poor. For those who are especially vulnerable to the lack of minimum levels of welfare, housing, education, safety, or employment, and who are not saved by the market, private charity, or statutory governmental programs, the Constitution offers no direct protection. It is difficult to see what sorts of concessions were actually extracted by the most poor from the better-off, whether or not embodied in the Constitution, that sufficiently compensate the poor for the absence of any constitutional recognition of their most basic practical interests.

Applying the logic of morally binding consent, we see that the abject poor are not morally bound by any purported consent on their part to the current Constitution. This conclusion can be supported by close analogy to ordinary contract law. Such a determination is, on an obviously larger scale, similar in basic respects to the familiar judicial practice of inquiring into what lawyers call the possible unconscionability of an ordinary contract. The general logic of unconscionability can easily be applied to our special concerns.

Consider, for example, the classic discussion of contractual unconscionability in the case of *Williams v. Walker-Thomas Furniture Co.*: "Unconscionability has generally been recognized to include an absence of meaningful choice on the part of one of the parties together with contract terms which are unreasonably favorable to the other party."[1] To determine unconscionability we must ask whether, at the time of contracting, there was an excessive disparity in bargaining power between the parties, and whether the substantive contractual terms were reasonably fair.

Plainly, the desperately poor have historically lacked, and continue to lack, anything remotely approaching bargaining power comparable to that of the better off. The poor have little to offer or with which to threaten, and have few resources and alternatives. Even if we assume that the poorest somehow participated in the constitutional drafting process, and that their relatively great vulnerability does not allow the better-off to simply wait them out in any negotiation, most of the poor do not have and perceive some practical alternative to consenting to the current Constitution.

This is not to suggest that differences in bargaining power by themselves suffice to set aside all or part of any contract. A contract that genuinely promotes the interests of the weak need not be set aside because of bargaining power differences between the contracting parties. At least some degree of "substantive" unconscionability embodied in unfair contractual terms should be required as well. Interestingly, however, the courts do not generally require a showing of both a great difference in bargaining power and extremely unfair substantive contract terms for unconscionability; a greater degree of either may make up for a smaller degree of the other. Of course, in our context, it is not difficult to detect a great degree of both.

The doctrine of unconscionability may provoke many questions. It is natural to wonder, for example, how the courts have historically validated agreements in the form of treaties entered into between the United States and various Native American tribes. One approach, apparently, has been to admit that at least some such treaties were coercively imposed on Native Americans with little bargaining power. Courts then save the agreement by presuming congressional benevolence and relying on a rule of construction that such treaties, where ambiguous, should be construed in favor of Native American rights and interests.

It is tempting to respond in detail to the astonishing sense of history, sound contract doctrine, and sheer complacency underlying such an approach. We shall, however, merely note its irrelevancy to our specific concerns. Even if a government, with or without justification, thus anoints its own motivations toward the powerless, such a presumption of official benevolence cannot cover our case. We are concerned with a social contract or constitution that may itself establish a government. To assume not merely a government, but governmental benevolence at this stage is irrelevant or question-begging. Some might argue that if it is reasonable to assume governmental benevolence toward Native American tribes, it is also reasonable to assume that the better-off private citizen drafters and ratifiers of the Constitution were sufficiently benevolent toward the excluded abject poor. But this argument, in addition to being dubious historically, simply assumes away most of the interesting issues. Given the essential absence of the most basic positive constitutional rights protection for the poor, we shall not make this assumption.

We should take a moment, as well, to note the inadequacy of allowing otherwise unconscionable contracts merely by construing any ambiguities in favor of the weaker party. The Supreme Court has typically not detected any relevant ambiguities in the constitutional text. Nor is this particularly surprising, given gross disparities in bargaining power and the absence of any real choice on the part of the poor. Generally, the powerful need not resort to, or tolerate, ambiguity. Those who are able to impose their will on others may be as direct and unambiguous in their constitutional drafting as they wish.

It is understandable, then, that the abject poor may abstractly prefer an enforceable basic positive constitutional right to the absence of such a right. But whether an abstract preference should reasonably translate into a refusal to consent to a constitution that generally provides for no such rights is a further, and complex, issue.

Our analysis in this respect must differ for every possible positive constitutional right. For illustrative purposes, let us focus initially on some form of a possible constitutional right to employment. Of course, such a right might be defined and enforced in many ways, and the costs and benefits of recognizing such a right would thus vary widely. But if we specify the nature and limits of a constitutional right to employment, the costs and benefits of such a right, to the poor and to the wider society, can be clarified sufficiently for rational choice.

The Supreme Court has not, even in its most expansive moods, remotely approached constitutional recognition of any general right to employment, even for adults eager and able to work. The American historical record is not utterly without support for some sort of right to employment on some terms. The American revolutionary patriot Thomas Paine, among others, was interested in such an idea.[2] But the Supreme Court, in implicitly denying any such right, admittedly is not resisting an onrushing tide of legal or popular opinion.

This may be due in part to historical and dominant cultural reasons. At the time of the ratification of the Constitution, and even of the post-Civil War amendments, land suitable at least for subsistence agriculture was widely available. Self-sufficiency may thus at the time have seemed a realistic alternative, under the circumstances, to private or public employment. And of course, independence and self-reliance have long been thought central to the American ethos and to civic virtue.

Whether the contemporary abject poor would reasonably prefer the absence of any constitutional right of employment is another matter. Unemployment rates among the urban poor are chronically high. Federal programs, federal and state statutes, state constitutional provisions, private charity, and market structures and incentives address this matter, but have plainly not solved the problem. For the abject poor, there is no available close practical substitute for a constitutional right to employment.

One might argue, however, that for a variety of practical reasons, a right to employment or to welfare would nevertheless not be insisted on by the abject poor, or that such a right would, even from the standpoint of the poor, best be left as an underenforced constitutional norm. Many of the relevant arguments, in a slightly different context, are summarized by Cass Sunstein in the following terms:

> if it were to follow that welfare was constitutionally guaranteed, the result may be to burden other programs with a good claim to public assistance, to produce unemployment and inflation, and to undermine incentives for labor. Of course these issues are sharply disputed; but there is a real risk that a right would harm the very people whom courts are trying to protect.[3]

Sunstein notes as well the problems of definition and implementation that a general right to welfare would produce. And in general, any government powerful enough to enforce a positive constitutional right has the power in fact, even if contrary to constitutional commandment, to injure the poor in other respects.

How should the abject poor respond to such arguments in considering whether to consent to a constitution that omits an employment right, or welfare rights in general? Employment rights by their very nature may not undermine incentives to labor as much as other sorts of welfare provisions might. One is, after all, merely being offered a real chance to labor. It seems advisable to begin by focusing narrowly on employment rights and briefly exploring the logic of insisting on such a right.

The costs of involuntary long-term unemployment are, of course, commonly high in any number of respects. Many important psychological, social, and material goals are attainable through work. Some of these goals can be obtained without work, as in play, hobbies, study, or a guaranteed income apart from work. Some jobs may be so horrifying that they do not contribute to some of these goals. But the vital social, communal, and psychological values commonly dependent on employment, and lost through chronic involuntary unemployment, are obvious. Nor are the substantial psychological costs of involuntary unemployment confined solely to the unemployed person. Most directly, families are affected as well.

The psychic costs of unemployment cannot easily be traced with precision. But it is not surprising, for example, that "[u]nemployed people experience higher levels of depression, anxiety, and general distress, together with lower self-esteem and confidence."[4] Admittedly, some of the psychic costs of unemployment may well be reduced precisely among the most poor, or in geographic areas of highest unemployment. There may well be less stigma in being unemployed if many neighbors are as well. But to a poor person choosing among constitutions, the prospect of reducing one's loss by comparing oneself solely with one's similarly abject reference group should be of limited appeal.

It is sometimes thought that we are rapidly becoming a knowledge-based society, in which the employment market will afford fewer opportunities to those without technical or professional skills. The market will, on such a view, come to regard increasing numbers of persons as permanently economically irrelevant. But almost no one wishes to be thought of as unnecessary and dispensable. The psychic costs of unemployment would largely remain even if it became clear that our economy is generating insufficient jobs for the poor.

For most poor persons who are thought of socially as potential breadwinners, prolonged involuntary unemployment means the absence of dignity, denial of a widely valued cultural role, powerlessness, the denial of status, a diminished identity, and the denial of a crucial opportunity to contribute and feel useful to the wider society. Here, welfare checks or a guaranteed income clearly provide no adequate substitute. And for the abject poor, the realistic choice is not between a constitutional right to employment and the strong practical probability, if not the formal guarantee, of long-term employment in the absence of such a constitutional right.

This does not fully answer the concerns raised by Sunstein. In the absence of the proverbial free lunch, the poor and the wider society would pay a real price for any enforceable constitutional employment right. Not all the costs result from strategic game playing and manipulation by the better off. While employment rights might reduce some welfare and medical care costs, there is doubtless some trade-off between the meaningfulness or attractiveness of the jobs guaranteed and inflation, taxes, public indebtedness, and funding for other sorts of welfare and other public programs of concern to the poor.

In some ways, any right to employment might thus harm the poor themselves, at least in some indirect fashion. But for many of the otherwise abject poor, the most crucial trade-off may be between such government-guaranteed employment on the one hand, and being unemployed in a somewhat wealthier and more productive economy on the other. If for no other reason than basic dignitary concerns or the desire to feel valued and useful, most poor persons may reasonably deem the benefits of such a right to substantially outweigh its costs and risks over the short and long term.

Of course, it is impossible to separate questions of the size and distribution of the costs of such a right from questions of the precise definition or scope of the right, on paper and in practice. The consequences of different rules will, in predictable and unpredictable ways, plainly differ. We may assume that the more attractive or dignified the job, the greater the social costs in other respects. The greater the job choice offered to each potential worker, the greater the costs. Increasing employment may tend to increase the cost of daycare, unless many of the new jobs are as daycare providers. Full-time employment may be more costly than part-time employment. Intuition suggests that wage subsidies, at least in the case of jobs that would otherwise really not be filled, may be less costly than pure non-market-oriented government jobs. But it may be hard to compare the social benefits of subsidized private market employment with, say, public employment in creating or maintaining basic infrastructure. Other questions then arise. How should we respond to the possibility that some sorts of jobs may tend more strongly to create additional employment than other sorts of jobs? Is there to be a class of persons officially deemed willing, but somehow "unable," to work? How should education and job training fit in? What sorts of behavior indicate an employee's real unwillingness to work or continue working?

A further complication is the possibility that jobs for, say, the last 20 percent of the involuntarily unemployed may be disproportionately socially costly. The abject poor generally might accept a constitutional right to employment that is not universal, but that practically guarantees employment for, say, 80 percent of the abject poor. Such a rule would significantly advance the prospects of the typical abjectly poor person, and would likely be more attractive to the poor than, say, a vaguer guarantee of governmental "best efforts" or "reasonable efforts" to maximize employment. It would, however, fail to make a categorical commitment to the dignity and value of each person, and this may be important, even apart from the remaining risk of falling into the 20 percent of unlucky unemployed among the abject poor. A rule that sacrifices 20 percent of the involuntarily unemployed sends a devaluing message even to the more fortunate 80 percent.

If the government adopts some "mixed" public and private employment strategy for fulfilling a right to employment, further problems of coherent meshing and perverse incentives arise. If government is to be the employer of last resort, the trick will be to provide government jobs that at least modestly fulfill the reasons for preferring employment in the first place, while not being so attractive by comparison with private sector jobs that the poor are drawn artificially and inefficiently toward government jobs.

Finally, the courts will inevitably be required to draw some sorts of judicial lines, precisely or vaguely, in this area. The issues raised will doubtless seem complex. But they may actually be no more complex than, say, the issues involved in formulating manageable state constitutional guarantees of a right to an education, or in adjudicating eligibility for workers' compensation, unemployment compensation, welfare benefits, or social security benefits.

Ultimately, the abject poor must ask whether the necessary complexity is worth the benefit. They should not, and presumably will not, feel bound to simply ratify the workings of current macroeconomic policy and the market. The market may prefer an outcome in which there are a few highly productive workers to an outcome with a larger number of admittedly less productive workers. There is a sense in which the former arrangement may be more "rational," in the sense of overall wealth-maximizing, than the latter. But there is no reason to expect the poor to sacrifice their own basic dignity and self-respect for the sake of promoting this narrow vision of rationality. Basic dignitary considerations provide good reasons to "artificially" subsidize employment rates. It is perfectly reasonable to prefer a society in which all contribute if they wish to a slightly "richer" society that declares some of its members involuntarily inconsequential.

Obviously, a right to employment is only one, and in some respects not an utterly typical, possible form of positive constitutional right. The difficulties of framing and implementing such a right cannot be denied. But it is important to focus on the central issue. Our concern is not, at least directly, with whether a right to employment, or any other welfare right, is popular with a stable middle class that knows itself to be middle class, or whether the mass of citizens is eager to pay the costs of implementing a right they themselves likely will never exercise. Such groups may be preoccupied with economic concerns of their own. Instead, our focus is on the possible obligations of the abject poor under the Constitution, and on whether such persons would reasonably consent to a Constitution as nearly devoid of welfare or other basic positive rights as is ours.

Bearing in mind the degree of freedom and information necessary for making such a morally binding choice, we may conclude that the abject poor would reasonably prefer some provision for basic constitutional welfare rights over its absence. This is not to unduly homogenize the thinking of the abject poor. Even given all the conditions of genuinely morally binding choice, some might prefer the absence of any such guarantees. Others might withhold consent because of the absence of, say, an employment right, while still others might be indifferent to an employment right while insisting on some other basic welfare right.

Consenting or refusing to consent to our current Constitution, however, seems to presume some benchmark or "baseline" situation, prior in logic or time, from which persons may or may not choose to "enter into" the current Constitution. How should such a prior baseline be conceived? We may think of such a baseline as the default position, as the one or more alternatives to consenting to the current Constitution, or as the "no agreement" point. But these are merely verbal descriptions.

Substantively, we might think of the pre-consent "baseline" as some political state of affairs that protects traditional property and liberty rights, but does not protect any basic welfare rights. But this would be largely question begging. Why should the abject poor be morally bound by a choice between two essentially similar possible regimes, where both regimes are indifferent to their basic interests? What good grounds exist for supposing that the abject poor would have freely consented to the prior state of affairs that is now deemed the morally relevant baseline? Are we to simply assume that their abject poverty or lack of bargaining power in the relevant baseline situation was deserved or somehow morally unobjectionable? In particular, are the continuing effects of slavery, segregation, or discrimination deserved?

Alternatively, we might think of the relevant baseline as some sort of prepolitical state of nature, without any territorially sovereign government. Whether such a state of affairs is of sufficient moral standing to serve as the baseline, or is even logically coherent, let alone practically realizable, is doubtful. How each of us would be faring in such an assumed state of nature will seem either impossible to tell or morally irrelevant. Should the naturally myopic simply be taken advantage of? Even our basic traits, abilities, and preferences reflect prior social arrangements. But one interesting observation may be made. It is certainly possible that most of today's abject poor would prefer their current status to a Hobbesian or even a Rousseauian state of nature. But in certain respects, the difference between their current lives—consider, for example, the chronically homeless—and a traditionally conceived state of nature, or even life under a tyrannical government, may not be enormous. Homelessness is in crucial respects not much worse than Hobbes.

If it comes down to bargaining over possible constitutional positive rights between the abject poor and the well-off, and if failure to agree on a common constitution is thought, however unrealistically, to plunge both rich and poor alike into a common state of nature, the rich plainly have a great deal further to fall, in theory, than the poor. That the well-off have so much more to lose if nonagreement means a state of nature would, again in theory, ironically provide a certain bargaining leverage to the poor. Of course, the well-off might not freely consent to any constitution that provides for basic positive rights. We may assume that the "leverage" or bargaining strength allowing them to hold out is entirely morally deserved, or not morally objectionable, and that their relative advantages arose without unfairness. But the unwillingness of the better-off to agree to any constitutionally basic positive rights merely sets up the whole problem of possible valid consent by the poor, and certainly does not resolve it.

Finally, we more neutrally might envision a complicated baseline that actually consists of a range of alternative constitutional regimes. Some regimes would provide for and others would deny any constitutional welfare rights. We may conclude that many of the abject poor would choose to consent, if at all, only to one or another of the constitutions providing for one or more welfare rights. We might further complicate matters by imagining the poor, perhaps along with the nonpoor, agreeing to some sort of procedure in which a random choice is to be made among two or more possible constitutions, some percentage of which would involve basic positive rights. But this would, for our purposes, lead to complication without enlightenment.

It must at this point be recalled that we are not arguing for or against constitutionally basic positive rights, generally or in connection with interpreting our current Constitution. Our point is merely that the Constitution has not been, and does not seem soon likely to be, interpreted or amended to provide for such positive rights, and that it is difficult to see why the abject poor would freely and knowledgeably consent to a constitution that makes essentially no provision for such rights.

It thus seems fair to conclude that even if consent theory is otherwise generally viable, no plausible version of consent theory can establish an obligation on the part of the abject poor to adhere to or be morally bound by the Constitution. This result is of special importance since, as we have seen, our constitutional system is commonly, if not officially, assumed to be based precisely on consent.

Perhaps it is possible, however, to completely set aside consent theory, and still hold the abject poor to be morally bound by the current Constitution. Other general approaches to the problem of constitutional obligation are possible. Among the most common are approaches based on considerations of gratitude, "fair play" or reciprocity, and the requirements of an alleged natural law. Each of these broad families of theories may be subject to basic general criticism.[5] We will again assume, however, that each of these theories is capable of grounding a moral obligation to obey in at least some circumstances. But our focus is not so broad. We are concerned with whether the abject poor can reasonably be thought bound. And it is ultimately implausible that the abject poor could be morally bound to the current Constitution through any appealing version of a theory based on gratitude, fair play or reciprocity, or natural law. It cannot be denied that gratitude, fair play, and natural law theories come in many varieties. Some varieties may be quite expansive in finding an obligation to obey. But the basic logic of these approaches cannot convincingly be stretched so as to bind the abject poor as a group.

It is not possible in a short space to discuss all possible variants of these three approaches to obligation. But neither is it necessary. Let us consider first the case of gratitude. Generally, plausible gratitude based theories cover cases where someone has been distinctively benefited by another person. Normally the benefactor has provided, out of a motive of generosity, more than what is legally or morally due and owing to the beneficiary. A gratitude theorist would thus have to argue, for example, that while the abject poor were and are largely unrepresented in the process of constitutional drafting and interpretation, and may occasionally take up residence in discarded refrigerator cartons, the government or the Constitution gratuitously provides distinctively more than what is morally appropriate for the poor to receive. The properly grateful response of the poor would then have to include adherence to the Constitution. This much cannot be plausibly claimed. Even if there are such things as legally enforceable obligations of gratitude, the abject poor plainly owe no such obligation to anyone in a form that can be properly discharged only by general adherence to the Constitution.

Fair play or reciprocity theories generally argue that we should not take unfair advantage of some ongoing more or less fair or legitimate common scheme by refusing to repay benefits we have received. The theory has it that we reciprocate by contributing our obedience and other elements of our fair share to that scheme. Thus if we have benefited from a volunteer fire brigade, or even if we have merely stood to benefit from that scheme, we should reciprocate by not riding free, and by appropriately contributing to and cooperating with the volunteer fire brigade scheme as an ongoing institution. Such theories tend to rely crucially on a logically prior sense of what is fair and unfair. But in the case of the abject poor, we may doubt whether, for example, typical residents of refrigerator cartons, even if they do not actively contribute to the constitutional scheme, can reasonably be described as exploiting or taking unfair advantage of that scheme.

Perhaps the problem can be restated. To say that the abject poor would be taking unfair advantage of our constitutional scheme by failing to recognize themselves as bound by that scheme is to again raise the question of why the present constitutional scheme is chosen as the crucial normative baseline. The underlying scheme requiring fair play must itself be reasonably fair. Why may we not imagine a constitutional scheme that accords more positive rights to the poor, and then ask about benefits and contributions? Can we say that the homeless are better off because of presumed general benefits such as an expensive military? Did the homeless benefit from past federal programs now being paid for through interest payments on the federal debt? Let us assume that the current size of the defense budget, along with all other government programs, is of some net value to the abject poor, above and beyond the sales and other taxes they unavoidably pay. What if many of the abject poor sincerely deny that such a net benefit is large enough to make their general obedience worthwhile? Many things are beneficial, yet not worth their cost of production. Shouldn't the government bear the burden of proving them wrong, since it is the government that proposes to coerce their obedience? No plausible fair play theory can simply reward those groups powerful enough to impose their will on others by uncritically making the current constitutional scheme the sole baseline for judgment.

Finally, natural law theories of obligation tend to emphasize the underlying objective moral logic of accepting the authority of the Constitution, based crucially on the moral status of the Constitution's substantive norms and ratification process. It is possible in principle to imagine some natural law theory that would hold the abject poor bound to the current Constitution, even if the poor were largely excluded from it, procedurally and substantively.

Such a natural law theory, however, would be implausible. The most plausible versions of natural law theory tend to emphasize human flourishing, basic human goods including avoiding disease and death, and the common good. Classically, Thomas Aquinas argues, for example, that the natural law requires that what we have in excess be transferred to the poor. Whatever one thinks of the details of such arguments, it is difficult to square the general absence of constitutionally basic positive rights with the health, other basic goods, and general flourishing of the abject poor. What we know about nature tells us that homelessness and chronic malnutrition do not generally promote human flourishing. Nor is it plausible to argue that promoting the minimal flourishing of the abject poor would typically cost us our own minimal flourishing.

Thus we may generally conclude, first, that no form of consent theory can establish a moral obligation to obey on the part of the abject poor. This is a crucial result, in that our Constitution is normally thought to be based on consent. Beyond this result, we may further conclude that none of the most commonly cited alternative approaches to obligation, including gratitude, fair play, and natural law theories, can plausibly be thought to bind the abject poor to the Constitution.

If the abject poor are not morally bound by the Constitution, what are they, the federal government, and the more privileged citizenry morally licensed or required to do? We should note first that the problem cannot be entirely confined to the federal constitutional level. As we have seen, at least some state constitutions are more protective of one or more basic positive rights than is the federal Constitution. But there is no reason to suppose that all state constitutions are sufficiently regardful of the interests of the abject poor as to have earned binding authority over them. One might then ask about the moral status of familiar state and local legislation, but this issue becomes inseparable from the problem of the scope of morally permissible options available to the abject poor with respect to the federal Constitution.

In an attempt to tackle this broad problem of the legal and moral status of the now constitutionally unbound abject poor, we might start from the perspective of the constitutional regime. That regime is, on our argument, confronted with a choice between beginning to sufficiently accommodate the interests, moral rights, and moral status of the abject poor, or else admitting its moral illegitimacy with respect to such persons. We shall, for the sake of the argument, assume that the regime does not choose the former course of reform and legitimacy.

This does not mean, however, that the public and the constitutional order can make absolutely no moral claims on the abject poor. Not all legitimately binding moral restraints depend on a legitimately binding constitutional regime. To explore this issue we must switch our perspective, and ask more concretely about moral limits on the actions of the abject poor under a constitutional order that is, at least as to them, illegitimate.

Here, it is difficult to place the abject poor within any familiar legal category. They are not, as a class, like visitors, immigrants, prisoners of war, enemy soldiers, foreign citizens, foreign sovereigns, criminals, wards, children, spies, quarantined medical cases, diplomatic representatives, voluntary or involuntary trespassers, or abductees. Nor are they necessarily civil disobedients, revolutionaries, or conscientious objectors. At least some of the abject poor may seek merely to make do as best they can, promoting their interests within whatever moral limits seem appropriate.

To see that some such moral limits still obtain, and that the constitutionally unbound abject poor do not, on our analysis, wind up with a blanket exemption from all moral standards, consider that there are contemporary theorists who believe that no one, rich or poor, bears any general moral obligation to obey any government. Such writers always go on to stipulate that there may well be good moral reasons, independently, for frequently acting the way the law requires. Even for those for whom the law in general is not morally binding, there remains a moral rule against rape, for example.

Of course, it is possible to deny that anyone ever has a moral obligation to obey, yet to hold the rich within much narrower moral limits than the crudely disenfranchised and the outcast. But some residual moral limits still bind even the abject. It is morally permissible for the abject poor to reasonably resist, for example, calls for them to simply leave the country, or to serve in a cynically intended way as mere cannon fodder in some military conflict from which they could not conceivably benefit. In view of what we have concluded to be their status, such impositions on the poor would simply be illegitimate.

But not all governmental mandates are like these. The Constitution and other laws also serve some almost pure coordinating functions, without serious conflicts of interests, but where violation of some coordinating rule or convention may impose substantial costs on innocent parties. If everyone else passes on the right, it will normally not be appropriate for the unbound abject poor to flout that convention, to the injury of others. This would hold at least if we set aside cases of what we would otherwise call conscientious civil disobedience. The broader law also forbids crimes such as rape, and the obligation to obey a legitimate regime is only the least of reasons for refraining from rape.

What, then, sets the precise limits on any special moral exemption held, on our analysis, by the abject poor? Inescapably, this question becomes quickly entangled with much broader issues of moral and legal philosophy. We cannot here consider such broader issues beyond a few brief comments. Those generally sympathetic to utilitarianism might urge the abject poor to follow cost-benefit considerations or rules in determining how to promote their interests. Presumably, utilitarianism would commonly underwrite an improved position for the abject poor, all else being equal, as long as we assume that a dollar transferred from the rich to the poor benefits the poor more than it harms the rich. After all, a dollar may make the difference between hunger and a meal for the abject poor. It is not easy to see how a dollar could make a comparable difference in the life of the well-off, but we will not insist on the point.

If we instead decline to apply a utilitarian approach, we might focus on some set of alleged moral rights and duties applicable in the circumstances of the abject poor. Given the range of possible rights theories, we cannot say much about the limits on what the poor may morally do without endorsing some specific approach to moral rights.

One crucial point, however, must be borne in mind. If the Constitution does not morally bind the abject poor, the legitimate options available to the poor can hardly be exhausted by traditional electoral and reformist mechanisms, coupled with reliance on the market and private charity. Let us recall that Thomas Aquinas, a writer who did not casually undervalue the rule of law, held that urgent, basic human need itself actually rewrites property rules. Aquinas concluded that

> if the need be so manifest and urgent that it is evident that the present need must be remedied by whatever means be at hand, ... then it is lawful for a man to succor his own need by means of another's property, by taking it either openly or secretly, nor is this properly speaking theft or robbery.[6]

Once we recognize that we cannot legitimately bind the abject poor to the current constitutional regime, the logic of this and similar self-help mechanisms becomes clear to the government, the better-off, and the abject poor themselves. The government would then confront a choice among general options. The first option is to illegitimately repress or make more difficult recourse by the abject poor to morally legitimate self-help mechanisms. The second option would be to seek to legitimately guide the exercise by the abject poor of such mechanisms and to reduce their cost to the better-off. The third and final option for the government is to move in the direction of achieving constitutional legitimacy with respect to the abject poor.

The following chapter assumes, in effect, that the basic circumstances of the abject poor, or those we may call the most deprived, have not changed for the better but that the government is nevertheless somehow morally legitimate with regard to such persons. Thus the following chapter's logic is utterly independent of the success or failure of the logic of this chapter. The argument of the following chapter may possibly stand, even if the argument of the present chapter is entirely mistaken.

The Progressive Logic of Criminal Responsibility

and the Circumstances of the Most Deprived

We know that the pull of gravity differs on the earth and on the moon. Can the pull of moral and social gravity also vary with place, even within what is nominally the same society? This chapter will argue that it can.

Legal systems have long assumed that humans, unlike the beasts and the angels, are commonly able to become whatever they wish. In particular, the law typically requires moral responsibility for criminal acts. Except in narrow standard categories of exceptions, as in cases of insanity, defendants are assumed to bear moral responsibility. It has been assumed as well, however, that it would violate our Constitution to impose punishment that is completely disproportionate to the offender's blameworthiness. There is remarkable agreement that in general, legal punishment for an act must not be imposed unless the defendant can be said to be blameworthy, or to bear moral responsibility for that act. Admittedly, we do have what are called "strict liability" crimes. In this narrow class, we criminalize, say, the selling of tainted jellies even if the seller was not careless or blameworthy with regard to the taint. But even these rare strict liability crimes assume that the defendant bears full responsibility for the decision to sell, or not sell, the jellies. In any event, the broad emphasis on responsibility leads our judicial system to frequently engage in self-contradictory behavior, typically at the expense of the most deprived members of society.

Certainly, the idea of responsibility is used in many ways. But there is a standard sense, relied on in the law, that can be called moral responsibility, and that is linked to moral blameworthiness. While we generally wish to avoid legal punishment, our capacity for bearing moral responsibility, for both good and bad acts, is often thought to be of enormous moral value. Immanuel Kant, for example, is well known for linking the capacity for rational decision making with dignity and moral value.

Whether all of us, all the time, would measure up to Kant's standards and thereby qualify as bearers of objective moral value is not entirely clear. Whether any of us is ever really capable of genuinely free, responsible, autonomous choice is a familiar philosophical question, lately complicated by fascinating debates over the possible relevance of quantum theory to free choice. There are risks, however, in failing to recognize some middle ground for human beings between completely free and autonomous reasoners on the one hand and mere "things" on the other. Let us all hope that if we only imperfectly meet the requirements of the former category, we will not be reduced to the latter. We may bear full responsibility even if we are not fully autonomous free reasoners. If, on the other hand, we credit all adult humans with rational freedom and moral autonomy, including those persons with the most horrific backgrounds and circumstances, we run another risk. We may in such a case be doing the victims of such remarkable deprivation no great dignitary favor. What is crucial is not whether the most deprived persons would be able to act autonomously if they were liberated from, or had never experienced, their severely constraining circumstances. Instead, what is crucial is the actual liberation itself of persons from those circumstances, and the eradication of such circumstances, so that the capacity for moral responsibility in other persons is not similarly stunted in the future. With the deeper philosophical questions, we need not further deal.

One related complication, however, deserves some attention. The law and many philosophers recognize "degrees" of responsibility. This is for some purposes important, but is not crucial to our concerns in this chapter. We may simply say that the law generally requires that the defendant bear some minimally sufficient degree of responsibility before criminal punishment for a particular crime becomes appropriate. Thus it is certainly possible for the law to convict two defendants of the same offense even if the defendants bore different degrees of responsibility for their separate acts. But even the less responsible defendant must have reached some baseline level of responsibility for the legal punishment to have been proper.

In this sense, criminal moral responsibility can for our purposes still be said to be an all or nothing affair. The law does, of course, recognize pleas of diminished responsibility. In criminal sentencing, the law also recognizes the possibility of mitigating and aggravating circumstances. Even among the most deprived, different persons are capable of different degrees of responsibility, and the same person may be capable of different degrees of responsibility at different times. Still, for our purposes it will generally do no harm to think of criminal responsibility as either present or not present in any given case.

Let us then begin to trace the logic and application of the well-established legal principle that only those who bear moral responsibility for an act should be legally punished for that act. As it turns out, there is a basic contradiction between the principle of no legal guilt without moral responsibility and the criminal law's disposition of an important class of defendants drawn from a group referred to here as the most deprived. This group is drawn from those who have most severely and persistently been deprived, through no fault of their own, of what we will see below to be the common material and social bases of moral responsibility. Briefly put, the criminal law systematically punishes substantial numbers of persons who, despite their failure to fall into any legally recognized category of excuse, on the standard view of responsibility cannot reasonably be said to bear moral responsibility for their charged conduct.

Generally, when the criminal law convicts those "most deprived" defendants who do not bear relevant moral responsibility, it does not recognize the contradiction in doing so. Instead, the law in practice often arbitrarily cuts off the inquiry into moral responsibility, thereby deforming and in practice abandoning the standard, generally accepted concept of moral responsibility itself. In doing so, the legal system commits a demonstrable, systematic error of logic and language use.

It is tempting to assume that matters must be more arbitrary than this. Surely it is impossible to convict the legal system of self-contradiction with any decisiveness. Determinations of responsibility are, after all, at least partly matters of normative judgments and politics. Whether a person or group is said to bear moral responsibility for an event is in practice subject to bargaining, which reflects differences in group power. Moral and legal ideas and language reflect power relationships. But it is an exaggeration to suppose that since imputing responsibility involves ideological or political struggle, legal practices regarding responsibility cannot be objectively shown to be self-contradictory. The logic of the concept of responsibility, as endorsed by the established legal system, may itself set important logical limits to the application of that concept, limits that may be demonstrably violated in practice by the legal system.

The idea of moral responsibility is in some sense at least partly a social construct. But this does not mean that the idea of moral responsibility is in all crucial respects arbitrarily alterable and infinitely manipulable by the better-off. Scientific ideas are, presumably, similarly human constructs. In particular, the idea of time and its measure are in a sense socially constructed. But this does not mean that the powerful can always, with consistency and credibility, accuse the weak of showing up five minutes late, even if it were always in the interests of the powerful to do so. Self-contradiction may still be possible. For some purposes, the powerful may want to say that anyone who shows up by noon, as calculated by a given method, is not late. The powerful may wish to seem fair. But by those very publicly endorsed criteria, some of the poor may show up by noon. This may be reasonably demonstrable. If so, the powerful engage in self-contradiction if they nevertheless rule all of the poor late. Once the principles of time, or of responsibility, are either discovered or merely settled upon, if only by the powerful, it becomes possible to convict the judicial system of using the relevant ideas inconsistently. This possibility becomes realistic because the judicial system, even if controlled by particular groups, typically seeks at least the appearance of fairness, justice across groups, evenhandedness, accuracy, reasonableness, and consistency.

If we think of moral responsibility as at least partially a social construct, that suggests that we should, as it were, take responsibility for the idea of responsibility itself. Why should we allow only particular groups to crucially formulate the authoritative idea of responsibility? But we would similarly bear responsibility for the idea of responsibility even if responsibility were as much inscribed into nature as

Planck's constant. If the idea of responsibility affects all of us, we all have an interest in scrutinizing critically the legal system's account of responsibility, even if we were to assume that the legal system claims to read off the idea of responsibility from the pages of nature itself.

Thus we need not argue that there is some single correct or objectively best understanding of the idea of moral responsibility, though we will offer some strongly redistributionist and egalitarian recommendations below. Instead our strategy is initially to convict current legal practices of self-contradiction, leaving unresolved for the moment how the self-contradiction should be remedied.

Exposing the basic self-contradiction at issue will absorb most of the remainder of this chapter. But it is easy to show how legal practices regarding moral responsibility may be self-contradictory, however politicized or non-rational they may be in other respects. Consider a legal system that generally rejects the idea of convicting defendants who do not bear moral responsibility for their acts, and that relies on our common, garden-variety understanding of what moral responsibility involves. Suppose that as a result of a political struggle, the law then decrees to be irrelevant any causal influences on the defendant's conduct that extend back further in time than one year prior to the alleged offense.

Plainly, there are now possible inconsistencies between the latter legal rule and our common understanding of moral responsibility. Suppose that two years prior to the offense, a third party successfully rewired the defendant's brain so as to dictate, unavoidably, only positive thoughts, inclinations, and motivations concerning a particular trespass. The rewiring required that the trespass be performed two years hence.

Of course, the defendant still can, under the legal rules, refer to her state of mind at the time of the offense, or within the prior year, which will in some limited sense admittedly be the relevant times. But the legal system cripples her ability to persuasively argue for her nonresponsibility at the time of the offense by barring her from introducing plainly logically and causally relevant evidence of any events earlier than one year before the crime. The point is not that the legal system's "one prior year" rule is a bad rule; rather, it is plainly inconsistent with the common understanding of the workings of moral responsibility, which the law still claims to uphold.

Thus it is possible not merely to object to a legal system's practices regarding responsibility on moral grounds, but to convict it of logical inconsistency. Legal systems may not only do bad things, they may also contradict their own premises. It is possible for the legal system's defenders to respond by merely casting uncontroversial and standard general understandings of responsibility aside, thus restoring internal consistency to the legal system. We will briefly explore the unattractiveness of such a possible response below. First, however, is the task of illustrating the actual contradiction in the legal system's claim to generally limit legal convictions to cases in which the defendant bears moral responsibility for the act in question, while convicting substantial numbers of the most deprived for acts for which they cannot reasonably be said to bear moral responsibility. Once that task is completed, we will briefly reflect on the attractiveness of an unusual combination of legal progressivism, egalitarianism, and concern for freedom with a strong emphasis on the moral value of responsibility. Such a combination, however uncommon, becomes possible once we fully recognize that responsibility depends on appropriate kinds and degrees of freedom, knowledge, and control.

There are two general senses in which it may be wrong to impute moral responsibility to some person. First, imputing responsibility may violate the accepted logic of the concept of moral responsibility. Even if moral responsibility were purely arbitrary and conventional, conventions may have their own logic. Second, the imputation may be unfair or unjust. Improperly imposing responsibility always violates the conceptual logic of responsibility, and in some cases may be unfair or unjust as well.

The "logic" of the concept of moral responsibility as used here is to be understood broadly. It includes all the criteria for the concept's proper application in actual legal practice. Thus by the "logic" of the concept of responsibility, we include not just misunderstandings of the meaning of the concept, but errors of fact or judgment in applying the concept as well. Assuming, for example, that starfish are as we ordinarily take them to be, to ascribe moral responsibility to a starfish is to a misunderstanding of the logic of the concept of responsibility. Of course, one can stipulate any meaning and any set of criteria for moral responsibility one cares to. But imputing responsibility to a starfish at least violates our conventional understanding of the idea of responsibility, whatever the point of violating such a convention might be. We also violate the logic of the concept of responsibility when we commit errors of fact or judgment in applying the concept, as, for example, in cases of mistaken identity, convictions for what we fail to see as involuntary acts, or when we mistakenly believe a causal relationship to exist between a defendant's activities and some social harm.

The case of attributing moral responsibility to a starfish illustrates the possibility of illogical, but not unfair or unjust, attributions of moral responsibility. Typically, it will be logically wrong, in the sense of confused or contradictory, to morally blame starfish, though not wrong in the sense of being unjust. Even if it is possible to treat starfish unjustly at all, or to genuinely punish or blame them, imputing moral blame to starfish, or mushrooms, or emeralds, does not itself seem unjust. Judging someone unfairly or unjustly seems to presuppose that the object being judged has a certain status, capacities, or actual or potential interests, to which the starfish cannot reasonably aspire.

It is certainly possible that the distinction between illogical and unjust ascriptions of responsibility is imperfect. Logic may not be completely separable from fairness. Commonly, judgments of responsibility will depend on normative judgments of what it is reasonable to expect of defendants. It may be that the broad logic of responsibility, as we ordinarily use the term, itself normally involves certain considerations of justice or fairness. The logic of the concept of responsibility may, for example, involve making judgments as to what is reasonable to expect of persons in particular situations. What is reasonable to expect may depend heavily on what is fair to expect. Holding the most deprived to be responsible or not responsible thus may require normative judgments.

Still, it is important to bear in mind the distinction between illogical and unfair imputations of responsibility. It may well be possible to show how particular impositions of responsibility are illogical or raise inconsistencies without resolving controversial broader issues of the fairness of the idea of moral responsibility or even the fairness of how it is being applied. Specifically, the judicial system may often commit self-contradiction in applying the logic of moral responsibility, even before any question is raised as to whether the system's current application or a consistent use of the idea of responsibility could somehow be unfair. This is important, in that we as a society may be able to agree or admit more readily that a concept is being applied inconsistently on its own terms than that a particular application of the concept would be fair or unfair. Detecting self-contradiction in judicial practice may thus be less controversial than claiming that the judicial system is in some respect unjust. And in addition, we may even be able to see the unfairness of holding some of the most deprived to be morally responsible before we can see, at a broader, more general and abstract level, that generally holding non-insane persons responsible may be unfair.

Of course, merely exposing contradictions in the logic of responsibility is not the end of the matter. If the logic of the judicial practice of moral responsibility is in some respect self-contradictory, it is still open to the judiciary, once it admits the contradiction, to abandon either of any given pair of mutually contradictory implications. It is therefore possible for the courts to resolve a contradiction in the logic of morally blaming by continuing to blame the most deprived defendants, while endorsing new, looser standards as to what counts as deserving moral blame. But there will often be pressures of politics, and even of logic and fairness, against repairing contradiction-riddled judicial practices of blaming merely by an ad hoc reduction in what the courts deem logically required for responsibility.

What, then, is the logic underlying judicial determinations of moral responsibility? The logic of responsibility refers to complex social practices in which conflicting social interests are crucially at stake, so we cannot expect the judicial logic of responsibility to be as crisp and uncontroversial as the logic of geometric cosines. There is, however, sufficient social and judicial consensus on the basic logic of responsibility to give rise to important contradictions between that basic logic and its application in legal practice. While understandings of the logic of responsibility will vary, at least in emphasis and detail, the logic of the concept is sufficiently clear for our purposes. Let us first briefly refer to the basic considerations, leaving detailed development for the discussion below.

Part of the consensus is that there clearly seems to be more than one simple element in properly imposing moral responsibility on criminal defendants. The idea of bearing moral responsibility seems to have no simple, unitary essence. Certain requisites of moral responsibility focus on the party's capacities, and others on the party's situation or circumstances. This contrast between capacities and circumstances is admittedly imperfect, as one's capacities and circumstances doubtless affect one another, at least over the long term. As we shall see below, other considerations relevant to responsibility seem to directly cut across the distinction between capacity and circumstance. Thus it seems clear that responsibility cannot be based on some single criterion.

It also seems clear by consensus that freedom, in some form and to some degree, is one requisite to moral responsibility. Interestingly, there seems to be roughly equal interest in volitional freedom, or freedom of the will, and in social freedom, which focuses on the number and value of the reasonably perceivable alternatives open for selection by the person concerned. This reference to freedom of the will is not meant to take sides between theories that emphasize the roles of causation and those that emphasize the role of character in questions of responsibility. In the sense in which we use the term, freedom of the will does not require that the crime was uncaused, or caused only by an utterly unconstrained personal decision.

On the capacity side, there seems to be a consensus that for responsibility to attach, the party must have some sufficient degree of relevant knowledge. This may require knowledge of the party's own capacities, or of external circumstances such as the availability, feasibility, or potential value of alternative options. The party as chooser must also possess some sufficient ability to predict the consequences of her own acts. Moral responsibility may not attach if the chooser knows that every choice will lead to only unexpected results.

On the circumstance side, there is often a sense that for moral responsibility to attach, some set of eligible alternative courses of conduct must have been available. As we will discuss below, the relationship between being morally responsible and having alternatives, or having the ability to do otherwise, is a bit more complicated. But the idea of available alternatives does seem generally relevant to responsibility.

The idea of control also commonly plays an important role in discussions of responsibility. Some degree of control over one's circumstances or options seems relevant to responsibility. Some degree of what might be called at least a capacity for self-control may also be relevant to responsibility. Control, from the standpoint of capacity, may also refer to the party's abilities to envision options, evaluate the options, and choose based on that evaluation. Some sufficient degree of each of these latter abilities is typically thought necessary for responsibility to attach. More deeply, it is commonly thought that the party to be held responsible must have had some sufficient ability to freely select, formulate, revise, and abandon even the basic values or goals that inform and give substance to that party's own choices.

We will consider and document a number of these criteria below. But it is important to note initially that we have not merely strung together a list of highly controversial assertions regarding the elements of moral responsibility. It is fair to say that much, if not all, of the preceding outline is at least compatible with most standard and commonsensical contemporary discussions of responsibility. Of course, many philosophers and some jurisprudes would wish to radically revise or abandon the idea of moral responsibility itself. We cannot address such concerns at length here, beyond pointing below to the likely unattractive consequences of such views.

Let us begin documenting the idea of responsibility in more detail by considering the relationship between freedom and responsibility. As we have seen, a distinction is often drawn between social or political freedom on the one hand and freedom of the will on the other. The first few lines of the Introduction to John Stuart Mill's essay *On Liberty* are devoted to just this distinction. No doubt social or political freedom and freedom of the will are in some sense distinguishable. For our purposes, we need not assume that there is a freedom of the will in a radical sense, consisting of utterly uncaused choices. Freedom of the will may, for our purposes, be thought compatible with some kinds of causal influences, if otherwise the will is still sufficiently free. But if our present concern is, unlike in the case of Mill's essay, primarily for understanding moral responsibility, separating social or political freedom from freedom of the will would be a serious mistake. Freedom of the will is typically linked to moral responsibility, and, crucially, freedom of the will often depends upon social and political freedom. Neither of these sets of linkages is universal or invariable. Admittedly, it is possible that we could prefer to live in a liberal democratic, politically free society even if we are all just organic robots utterly lacking in free will. But it is clearly possible that the denial of social and political freedom to a group of persons may tend to undermine freedom of the will, and ultimately the capacity for moral responsibility, of that oppressed group. One of the principal errors embedded in contemporary criminal justice and sentencing is the judicial refusal to recognize the significance of the linkage between social or political freedom and freedom of the will.

Part of the problem may stem from the fact that defendants can sometimes be properly held morally responsible for outcomes that they did not intend, as in negligence cases. But some acts unintentionally inflicting harm may be performed with free will. Although we can be responsible for some unintended outcomes, it does not follow that we can be responsible for outcomes that do not at any point reflect free will. Even when a legal system holds an addict responsible for an act not reflecting the addict's free will, it is typically presumed that free will was relevantly exercised by that party at some earlier time, particularly in a free choice to become, or risk becoming, an addict.

This dual aspect of freedom, encompassing both social or political freedom and freedom of the will, has been raised in discussions of moral and legal responsibility at least since Aristotle. For Aristotle, responsibility for an act requires not just the actor's knowledge of the circumstances, but a deliberate choice to undertake that act, as well as the absence of any external compulsion regarding that choice. Aristotle's insights linking both political and volitional freedom to responsibility have been preserved to the present day.

The importance of both political freedom and freedom of the will has been recognized by the contemporary philosopher Susan Wolf, for example. Wolf has observed that freedom and responsibility require not only the actor's "ability to govern her behavior in accordance with her deepest values," but the "ability to form or revise her deepest values in light of the truth."[1] After all, even one's deepest values may have been coercively implanted. And of course, the inability to act on our deepest values may reflect lack of political freedom. Wolf implicitly links the two sorts of freedom in noting that "[t]he more options and the more reasons for them that one is capable of seeing and understanding, the more fully one can claim one's choice to be one's own."[2] The linkage between the number of available options on the one hand and social or political freedom on the other reflects a familiar, commonsense understanding of freedom. Someone who may select from a range of choices is normally freer than she would be if she could select from only a much more limited set of those choices. Wolf then further requires that for responsibility to attach, the chooser must "understand the significant features of her situation and of the alternatives among which her choice is to be made."[3] This further requirement of knowledge and understanding may in turn take on an important social and political dimension, as we will argue below. It is hardly surprising that lack of political freedom may be linked to suppression of the unfree person's understanding of her own circumstances.

To similar effect is an argument raised by another contemporary philosopher, Gary Watson. Watson raises the possibility that persons subject to totalitarian mind control may "lack freedom . . . because their evaluational and volitional and other cognitive faculties have been impaired in certain ways. . . . [T]hey are incapable of effectively envisaging or seeing the significance of certain alternatives, [or] of reflecting on themselves and the origins of their motivations."[4] While Watson refers to dramatic hypothetical cases, we will argue below that the lack of freedom Watson describes may undermine the development of the capacity for responsibility among the most deprived members of contemporary society.

In the meantime, the linkage between social freedom and freedom of the will can be clearly seen through a simple hypothetical example. Consider the case of a person who freely wishes to do evil, but whose brain has been rewired, over her protests, to produce only socially approved moral motives and actions. Surely we would not wish to sever the link between social and volitional freedom by offering genuine moral praise, in the fullest sense, to such a person. It might be prudent for us to reinforce or publicize and reward such socially approved behavior, but moral praise for her socially approved actions clearly would not be appropriate in any deep, genuine sense.

It seems clear that coercive restrictions may not only affect the victim's social freedom, but may also impair the victim's capacity to bear moral responsibility for her acts and choices. Coercion can preclude or diminish moral responsibility. But it is also important to avoid the error of supposing that it is only coercion in some narrow sense that can undermine the sorts of freedom necessary for moral responsibility. Particularly in light of the diversity of approaches to the idea of coercion, it is crucial to bear in mind that freedom may be limited in a way that reduces the capacity for moral responsibility even if direct, narrow coercion is not applied. Government policy and legal practice may reduce freedom and the capacity for moral responsibility without, at least on some conceptions, employing coercion.

Consider, for example, that the idea of coercion is sometimes linked to the desire, of a specific party doing the coercing, that an identifiable target of the coercion respond with some particular action favored by and to the benefit of, usually, the coercer. Thus a robber who coerces a victim would prefer to receive the victim's money rather than carry out his threat to take the victim's life. But not all lack of social freedom is like this. A person may be unfree, in the sense of having, for social reasons, only starkly limited and distinctly unattractive realistic options, even if no one cares which of those few options the person happens to choose. After all, the fewer one's resources, the less likely it is that one has valuable assets anyone would be interested in obtaining through coercion. A society might limit the options of the most deprived without caring much about which option the most deprived actually choose. In such a case, at least some persons might say that no coercion is present.

In sum, sufficient social freedom is typically linked in practice to freedom of the will and to the capacity for moral responsibility. The linkage of freedom, both social and volitional, to responsibility is illustrated further in the linkages of knowledge and control to the idea of responsibility. In certain respects, knowledge and control must be present in order for a party to be held morally responsible, and one's knowledge and control can reflect one's freedom or lack thereof.

We have seen that Aristotle considered relevant knowledge a prerequisite to responsibility. This theme was developed classically and has been maintained in contemporary accounts of responsibility. For responsibility to attach, one must have sufficient relevant knowledge of the nature of one's own action, the surrounding circumstances, and the likely effects of one's act. Lack of knowledge thus tends to preclude responsibility. Of course, there may be cases in which an actor's ignorance is irrelevant or the actor's own fault. Ignorance of fact, possibility, likelihood, or moral and legal rules may in some cases be wholly or partly the fault of the party involved. This fault may be direct or indirect. In some cases, we may in effect hold a person responsible for their own current lack of responsibility.

Thus one may still bear responsibility for an act or outcome, even if one chose on the basis of gross ignorance, as long as that ignorance was one's own fault. More broadly, ignorance of the law is typically thought not to excuse, presumably on the grounds that one's failure to know what the law requires is in some sense one's own fault. But there are limits to the extent that an actor's ignorance can realistically be said to reflect the actor's own fault. Oppressed groups may, for example, nonculpably lack relevant knowledge, whether we wish to say that they have not acquired such knowledge, that government and society have failed, culpably or not, to provide such knowledge, or that government and society have not provided adequate opportunity to acquire such knowledge.

For responsibility to attach, the allegedly responsible party must know enough about the society's moral and legal code and perhaps about society's likely view of the moral and legal status of one's acts. At least the opportunity to learn must have been present. But the actor need not be capable of empathetically grasping or seeing the point of morality, or even of making genuine moral decisions. This is a controversial point. It has been argued to the contrary that only those who can make genuinely moral decisions for moral reasons can be held morally responsible. In particular, it has been argued that responsibility cannot attach in the case of an otherwise normal person who genuinely can see no distinction between moral rules and merely conventional, ultimately arbitrary rules of etiquette, and who sees both sets of rules as senseless.

These claims, however, are incorrect. Perhaps the quickest way to show that these arguments are, despite their apparent logic, ultimately implausible is to notice who is thereby excluded from the class of the morally responsible. Among contemporary academics, for example, there are some conscientious, sincere moral skeptics, nihilists, and others who consider themselves incapable of genuinely moral decision making, who see no difference between morality and arbitrary convention, and who fail to grasp, or who deny, any genuine point to morality. Yet it would plainly be wrong to conclude that all such academics cannot be held morally responsible for their actions.

Let us quite realistically assume that such academics are otherwise in possession of all the requisites of responsibility. While they deny or cannot genuinely understand, engage in, or be motivated by moral considerations, it is still reasonable to hold such persons morally responsible: given their otherwise normal if not superior capacities, they can grasp how the institutions of law and morality will likely evaluate acts they may be considering, and can easily refrain on that basis from such acts. If they are not motivated by any premoral sense of empathy, they may still be guided at least by self-interested prudence to appreciate the likelihood and undesirability of criminal punishment. At least some moral skeptics may excel at predicting how society and the legal system will evaluate their contemplated acts, and can easily refrain on prudential grounds from engaging in acts the society will predictably condemn. One might, by way of analogy, be able to predict what a group of astrologers would say in any given case, based simply on one's study and experience, even if one thinks that astrology is just so much malarkey.

The key step in this logic is that a legal system's reaction may be quite predictable, even if its reasoning is or is thought by the moral skeptic to be flawed or mysterious. Persons do not need a moral sense to develop a workable grasp of what a legal system will call a homicide. There are problems of legal indeterminacy, but they afflict morally motivated actors as well. Even if one sees no genuine moral difference between murder and self-defense, one can note the empirical correlates of self-defense, such as a prior shot by the attacker. To be on the safe side, one can simply avoid homicide generally. Consider the matter from an anthropological perspective. It is possible to accurately predict how certain nonmoral distinctions of a culture will be played out, based only on one's observations of that culture, even if one finds the distinctions to be mysterious. Similarly, if a society's moral or legal response to homicide forms a reasonably consistent pattern, even those who deny the logic of or are otherwise incapable of moral reasoning may grasp the likely consequences of apparently intending and causing the death of some unarmed stranger. Whether the law should then go on to equally punish persons who sincerely deny that the ideas of morality or moral responsibility make sense is another matter.

Thus even the moral skeptic professor may have a sufficient ability to act in accordance with what the mysterious although more or less predictable institutions of law and morality may require. What sets academic moral skeptics apart from those persons subject to the most serious oppression is that the former have, and the latter may sometimes lack, a reasonable and realistic opportunity to absorb and then uniformly apply in practice the majority's relevant legal and moral norms.

These considerations take us beyond what we have called the cognitive or "knowledge" prerequisites to responsibility, and into the related area of the "control" prerequisites to responsibility. Persons may lack relevant control over some of their own personal characteristics, over external facts and events, over their own substantive choices or process of choice, or over their own lives, and therefore bear reduced or no moral responsibility. One may, for example, lack control over one's own choice-making process for uncontroversial reasons, such as direct forceful coercion by another person or genuinely involuntary addiction, which in turn tend to negate the chooser's moral responsibility.

The legal system is thus confronted with a syllogism whose major premise holds that those relevantly lacking in control should bear reduced or no responsibility for their acts and choices. The same syllogism's minor premise holds that at least some of the most deprived lack such control. The conclusion of the syllogism therefore calls into question the responsibility of such persons. The legal system has generally avoided this conclusion by insisting that only a narrow set of nonsystemic, essentially personal or idiosyncratic excuses exhaust the conditions that preclude moral responsibility. Thus the legal system may, in assessing the criminal culpability of a defendant, consider whether the defendant is in a specified sense insane. The legal system is in practice, however, unlikely to go on to consider whether the sane defendant's grimly and involuntarily stultifying life circumstances have undermined any of the other logical elements of responsibility discussed above. Courts tend instead to make limited concessions to the logic of responsibility, at some cost in inconsistency, as when they admit evidence of the defendant's opportunities and capacities relevant to responsibility only in the context of death penalty sentencing.

While the legal system engages in crucial inconsistencies in this regard, even those philosophers who devote themselves to such questions also occasionally betray what might be called a certain class insensitivity in this regard. Philosophers tend to focus on hypothetical exotica such as hypnosis, involuntary drugging, and high-tech brain control without bothering to then test the extension of their results to more mundane social contexts. It is no doubt useful for certain purposes to focus initially on clear, depoliticized, isolated, uncontroversial cases. But too often the analysis is then extended, if at all, only into the familiar narrow categories of excuse. Even when philosophers consider broad concepts such as great strain or abnormal stress, they often reduce the significance of their own analyses by focusing on stress as an episodic, personal, or transient phenomenon, as opposed to the chronic, inescapable, systemic horrors faced by the most deprived groups.

It is true that even the most severely deprived criminal defendants may be quite sane, intelligent, creative, resilient, and resourceful. Bare survival under crushing circumstances may commonly require the latter. But these truths should not distract us from the various ways a person may be denied the capacity for genuinely bearing responsibility. Severe and prolonged environmental influences may impair the development and exercise of the capacities relevant to responsibility. One can be bright and creative and yet a tightly confined prisoner. It might be feared that if the most severely deprived persons can, for example, creatively adapt to their circumstances and yet not be capable of bearing moral responsibility, perhaps, in truth, none of us really bears moral responsibility for anything. This is of course a deep and long-standing question. We need not address it for our purposes simply because the law obviously makes no such assumption. As we will note below, relevant distinctions can be drawn, with respect to the conditions for developing the capacity for responsibility, between the circumstances of the well-off and the circumstances of the most deprived.

One final aspect of the "control" element of responsibility deserves some attention. The relationship between moral responsibility and freedom, in the senses of being able to act otherwise than one did, or of having open and available alternative courses of action, is not as clear as is sometimes imagined. As it turns out, interestingly, one cannot always infer lack of responsibility from the lack of all sorts of freedom.

Roughly speaking, we often assume that there can be no free will without open alternatives available for choice, or that freedom requires that the chooser have been able to choose otherwise. Similarly, it is often assumed that one can be held responsible only if one had the ability to refrain from acting as one did, or that responsibility can attach only if one had the ability to choose otherwise, setting aside cases in which one's inability to choose otherwise is one's own fault.

It may be, though, that moral responsibility can in some cases attach even where the actor was nonculpably unable to do otherwise, or where only one course of conduct was really open to that actor.

Though this may sound odd, clear examples are not hard to find. We might want to be considered responsible for our choice in favor of some huge moral and personal good over some literally repulsive moral and personal evil, even if we found ourselves in some sense unable to choose otherwise. There are also cases of overdetermination, in which, say, person A freely decides to murder B and does so unwaveringly, but where C has secretly implanted a device in A's brain that would inevitably have forced A to carry out the murder even if A had at some point decided not to. The lesson of such cases is that A can be morally responsible for murdering B, even if, given the implanted device, A could not have done otherwise. A would have killed B whether he revised his intentions or not.

For our purposes, we need not pass judgment on the merits of these arguments. Even if they complicate or sever certain linkages between certain sorts of freedom and responsibility, they do not seem to bear on the kinds of deprivation and unfreedom we examine below. They certainly do not establish the universal moral responsibility of the most deprived. The examples above work best when they assume a broadly free, knowledgeable agent exercising the relevant sorts of control. In the first case, the chooser is then "confronted" by the inescapable implications of her own autonomously chosen value system, "dictating" a choice. In the latter case, the actor carries out the murder in accordance with her free choice or else finds her free and responsible decision to change her mind being "overruled" or inhibited by the implanted brain device. These sorts of examples presume the kinds of freedom, knowledge, and control that we shall argue are often absent within the most severely deprived societal groups.

Before we move on to explicitly consider the circumstances of the most deprived, we must emphasize a crucial conclusion. The legal system cannot infer responsibility from the belief that even the most deprived persons act conscientiously and intentionally to obtain what they happen to see as their best outcome or to maximize their values. In a word, rational behavior in this sense does not imply responsibility. While even the poorest of the poor may act in a rational, adaptive, imaginative, or creative way, this does not imply their responsibility for their choices. One might do exactly this under the most severe and inescapable restrictions on one's choice. One might seek what one imagines the best payoff even if one is utterly unaware of how much one's capacities and options have been limited, or how one's own values have been unfreely arrived at. Someone, for example, who is being coerced by an armed robber may intentionally and rationally maximize her values by complying with the robber's demands. She may, even while acting under such extreme duress, creatively manage to improve her position in some way. Yet she may well not bear moral responsibility for acting as she does. Once we go on to recognize that not everyone's basic values are formed under conditions of equal freedom, responsibility becomes even more dubious.

It is not necessary, of course, to base a claim of the nonresponsibility of the most deprived on an assertion that government or society coerces their behavior. Any respect in which the most deprived nonculpably lack the necessary kinds and degrees of freedom, knowledge, and control undermines responsibility, even in the absence of any malicious intent by the broader society or coercion in a narrow sense. Nor is it decisive whether the most deprived feel responsible or happen to identify with their choices, under the circumstances. A deprived group may well be socialized to believe themselves to bear responsibility and to identify with their choices. A society's structural stability may depend on whether the least well off believe, rightly or wrongly, that their basic choices and values are freely arrived at. The question remains whether such persons are in fact responsible, and whether in identifying with their actions they have done so freely, or would do so under conditions of freedom.

We have thus far discussed what is necessary for persons to properly bear moral responsibility for their acts. We will now show that significant numbers of persons today lead lives that in crucial respects do not always meet those requisites of responsibility, but who are nevertheless systematically treated by the legal system as though they did. To show this in a genuinely convincing way would require a vivid portrait, true and whole, of the lives of the most deprived. No such ambitious task will, of course, be undertaken here. Instead, we will simply link up brief descriptions of relevant lives with the criteria for responsibility set forth above.

Our discussion will focus on those we have referred to as the most deprived. Obviously, this terminology itself involves elements of evaluation and comparison. The term has, at least, enough intuitive substance so that we cannot say that the "most deprived" bear or lack responsibility simply by their very definition. While the idea of the "most deprived" is obviously vague, it is evocative enough for our limited purposes. It is no more vague, and less pejorative, than possible alternatives, such as "lumpenproletariat" or "underclass."

In any event, it is recognized across the political spectrum that substantial numbers of persons are born into and live their lives amid conditions of remarkable deprivation, in comparison to the broader society. It is similarly a commonplace that people do not in any sense choose the basic features of their own initial nurturing, their family, or their own early environment. The impact of horrific environments can plainly be substantial, especially if one's resources for escaping or overcoming such an environment are quite limited. Of course, many members of the middle class and at least a few others may be tempted, for self-interested and other reasons, to deny the importance of such effects. Such a denial is, however, unreasonable. We may grant that some persons who are among the most deprived seem to accept full moral responsibility for their criminal acts. Such persons obviously know their own lives best. But it would hardly be

surprising if their own lack of knowledge and their general deprivation led them to not fully understand and appreciate how freedom,
knowledge, and control consitute responsibility. The most deprived
often live in a broadly punitive world. The ideological usefulness, to
dominant groups, of an inclination to self-reproach and self-blame
among the most deprived is obvious. Some persons face, from infan-
cy, and through no fault of their own, a frightening array of mutually reinforcing and largely unopposed negative forces, including isolation, threats, the absence of favorable models, social indifference,
drugs, impoverishment, aggressive gangs, neglect, abysmal early edu-
cational opportunities, and a local correlation of financial success
with illegality. The cumulative impact of these and other forces in
some cases overwhelms any more positive forces.

It is impossible to illustrate this phenomenon in such a way as to
convince the skeptical. It is too difficult for us to really grasp a world
in which, for example, a respected minister of religion can obtain
utterly unskilled employment for his charges only by essentially brib-
ing employers to take them on. Survival strategies in such a world
may involve, for example, concealing from the neighborhood that
one has made a major consumer purchase, through careful trash disposal patterns. Or one may seek to enhance one's physical security by
habitually offering cough drops to potentially threatening neighborhood drug users, as though their respiratory symptoms indicated the
presence of a cold. One might under such circumstances conclude at
a remarkably early age that survival requires, pathetically, that one
make as few friends as possible. Each of these examples is real.

In such a world, four- and five-year-old children may show up at
the neighborhood preschool with hats turned in one direction rather
than the other, indicating allegiance to one neighborhood gang
rather than the other. This is not to suggest that four- or five-year-
olds genuinely make choices among rival gangs. That is hardly the
point. Rather, we should attempt to vaguely imagine what seems

normal, what seems reasonable, and what seems reasonably feasible to that child, at that point and years later.

Those four- and five-year-olds may arrive at school with, in some cases, no familiarity with their own officially recognized name, names of colors, letters, or how to hold a pencil. Some have not only not been read to, they may not have been regularly talked to. This is not to blame fathers or mothers. That is for present purposes irrelevant. Later, they may aspire, perhaps, to become a doctor or lawyer while receiving Ds in school, or reading little beyond comic books. In such cases, there is an unappreciated mismatch between one's aspirations and the realistic limits on one's achievement.

This is a world in which vital medical prescriptions, necessary for the health of a premature infant, go unfilled or unused, perhaps for lack of funds, lack of transportation, lack of understandable explanation by medical professionals, or a general lack of ability or inclination on the part of the health professions to follow through on such matters. In such a world, the result may be a mother hysterically reacting to attempts by paramedics to physically pry away from her the eventually deceased infant.

But even if such circumstances and their effects could be vividly conveyed, the resulting image of life for the most deprived would still be far too benign and antiseptic. Consider the actual case of a newly appointed, but sophisticated and well-qualified, housing manager for the Henry Horner Homes in Chicago, a large public housing project that is by no means the most dangerous in Chicago. The well-intentioned newly appointed manager, upon making an inspection tour of the basements of the Henry Horner Homes, reacted, elementally, by vomiting, for understandable reasons the curious reader is invited to pursue independently.[5] Eventually, the newly appointed housing manager turned to other responsibilities.

These vignettes might be multiplied. But even if their bare recitation began to have a cumulative impact, the cumulation would eventually desensitize us to the alienness and sheer horrors involved, thus undermining the point. Suffice it to say that if we could genuinely grasp what it might be like to live one's entire life within such horizons and such constraints, we might well come to question the logic of invariably inferring moral blameworthiness by extending our own distinct experiences to cover theirs.

Ordinarily we hold persons criminally morally responsible if we conclude, metaphorically, that they have culpably turned away from the good, or closed their eyes to the presence of the good and its practical eligibility. This sort of assessment of human behavior is often accurate. But whether it is a fair and accurate characterization, invariably, of those among the most deprived who commit crimes is doubtful in the extreme. Even the greatest, most sympathetic, most sensitive and articulate literary depictions of the lives of the desperate may have an unintended counterproductive effect: they may lead us to believe that we fully grasp what it is like to be desperate, when of course no work of art can do this. Our reactions to artistic or literary depictions must always lack a dimension that would be present if we lived as, or even among, the most desperate. We fill in what is missing, if at all, with our own experiences. All descriptions of the poor are in this sense conservative in their impact.

Persons in such circumstances are, in many instances, subjected to conditions that strongly tend to preclude or impair responsibility, including lack of relevant freedom, lack of relevant control, and lack of relevant knowledge. Their lives are led in either real or reasonably and nonculpably perceived isolation from any institutions and opportunities that would permit escape from such an environment and its powerful influences.

In particular, the most deprived have, over the last few decades, found themselves increasingly isolated, informationally and geographically, from employment opportunities holding promise of a stable, economically conventional lifestyle. The trend toward relocation of industrial manufacturing jobs away from central cities is an important factor in this isolation. Nor has the cybernetic revolution broken this isolation of the most deprived. This economic isolation in turn reinforces a broader cultural isolation, which reflects, and in turn worsens, the elements of lack of relevant control, freedom, and knowledge of available escape routes and alternatives. The mere existence of some job, for example, does not imply that one knows about or reasonably can find out about that job, or that one is able to apply for and obtain transportation to and from that job, even if one were to qualify and be hired. The absence of sufficient relevant knowledge, freedom, and control is again crucial.

No doubt the existence of some limited number of virtually minimum wage jobs, without health insurance or other benefits, is within the reasonable scope of knowledge of even the most deprived. In a sense, every able-bodied person could be charged with a culpable failure to seize such opportunities. And there is a sense in which each of a large number of persons can be held accountable for not seeking and obtaining one of a small number of available such jobs, even if the ratio of unemployed persons to minimum wage job openings is such that most job seekers cannot possibly be accommodated. In a game of musical chairs, everyone can be faulted individually for not successfully finding a seat, even if there are far fewer seats than players.

The problem, however, is that it is widely believed by the most deprived, rightly or nonculpably wrongly, that such jobs cannot reasonably be expected to sustain or even lead to societal respect and the material foundation for a stable, economically conventional adult existence. This leaves many of the most deprived with either unrealistic hopes, abetted by national entertainment media, for dramatic financial success, or with a fatalistic sense that their lot in life has already been largely determined. Even where such a belief is false, those holding such a belief may not be culpable in so believing.

This subjective sense of lack of relevant control is widely thought by many observers to be largely realistic, and to reflect cultural and economic realities largely beyond the control of individual persons, however defeatist its implications. For those trapped by these realistic perceptions and realities, it would be unreasonable to pretend to mainstream status. Even if these beliefs are mistaken, that cannot itself serve as a general basis for ascribing responsibility to those reasonably holding such beliefs. And even if we have a deeply ingrained dislike of defeatism or pessimism, we cannot be unreasonable in our expectations of those who are among the most deprived. Their lives may tend to tell them a clear and distinctive story.

Many of the most deprived face, in addition to the constraints referred to above, coercion by peers, inadequate school curricula, one degree or another of continuing societal racism, and other more material sorts of barriers and constraints. Aside from the geographic, financial, qualification- or credential-based, or purely information-based barriers to particular jobs, the most deprived may for whatever reason simply not be wanted by the more desirable employers. Even if the most deprived were in a position to "hear" of appropriate job vacancies, employers commonly do not wish, or do not bother, to "speak" to such potential applicants. Suburban employers with even potentially accessible jobs to fill may not advertise their vacancies in any medium likely to reach the most deprived.

Even when the most deprived choose between apparently equally eligible options, as between remaining in school and leaving school, or between drug use and the avoidance of drugs, the choice may well be based on only minimal differences in moral or other value, even if the choice is not somehow constrained. It seems fair to conclude, for example, that much drug addiction among the most deprived reflects not an informed and unconstrained search for temporary gratification, but a much more negative sort of "choice": a sort of vague, lingering suicide for lack of a significantly more appealing alternative.

These considerations, then, admittedly quite inadequately illustrate some of the relevant dimensions of life for those we have called the most deprived. How, then, does life in such circumstances square with what we have seen to be the necessary elements of moral responsibility? There would appear to be substantial numbers of persons who live their lives in circumstances hostile or indifferent to those essential requisites of moral responsibility. Our making this judgment may require some normative judgments, as well as the exercise of pure logic. But not all normative judgments about moral responsibility are equally difficult and controversial.

Certainly, this is also not a matter of the mere predictability of anyone's actions. We cannot, admittedly, show that someone was not responsible for an act merely by successfully predicting that act. It may be predictable that most persons quietly offered a no-strings choice between two dollars or one dollar will choose the two. But mere predictability does not by itself imply any relevant sort of constraint. Some choices may simply be uncontroversial and exercised with full responsibility.

Conversely, we should not assume the moral responsibility of all of the most deprived merely because their choices differ substantially in apparently similar contexts. Persons who appear to have led similar lives may in fact have had relevantly different histories, influences, burdens, and resources. Small initial differences may be magnified or compounded into great differences at later stages. That the movement of a butterfly's wings may produce a hurricane does not mean that even the best meteorologists are able to trace the hurricane back to the butterfly. The observable differences in the background or history of those who can and cannot be held responsible for their acts most certainly need not be large.

At a very minimum, it is clear to begin with that some criminal defendants do not live in a world of risk-benefit calculations of any sort familiar to the rest of us. Consider, for example, an interesting detail within the account provided by Cornelius Singleton of his murder of Sister Ann Hogan in an isolated cemetery, a crime for which Singleton was eventually executed:

> I saw the nun about 1:30 when she came in the cemetery walking. . . . I walked on down to where she was. She had some beads on her hand, talking to herself [i.e., praying]. I came up to where she was and I told her my problem. The problem was about my old lady, Cathy and about us breaking up. She said she would pray for me and Cathy. I just wanted her to hurry up and get in touch with Cathy. She said she didn't have no transportation. I said, You know, can we get some. She said somebody brought her down there. All of a sudden, I got worried about Cathy. She started to walk off. I grabbed her around the waist and she fainted then. I picked her up and took her and walked into the wooded area with her. I laid her down on the ground and tied her up . . . . She had a little radio or something [i.e., a pager] clamped to her. I throwed it away in the cemetery. I believe I can still remember. I took a watch off her arm. It was silver. It was of no value. I had it in my hand and I took it to my grandfather's house and put it in the window.[6]

The watch in question eventually provided, not surprisingly, a portion of the physical evidence linking Singleton to the crime. We do not claim that Singleton's theft and disposition of the watch indicated insanity on his part, or the inappropriateness of morally blaming Singleton, though it is worth mentioning that Singleton's intelligence quotient was apparently measured at approximately seventy or less. We do not claim that Singleton fell within the category of the most deprived. Nor do we suggest that Singleton's crime is unusual because it is, at least from our standpoint, pointless, or even bizarre. As the distinguished observer of criminal behavior Sherlock Holmes once pointed out, crime is common and logic is rare. Leaving finger-prints on the pager is illogical to us. We wish to make only a more modest point: quite apart from any malice, depravity, or evil one might wish to ascribe to Singleton, his calculations of sheer self-interest simply do not track our own.

Notice in particular that Singleton describes the watch as of no value. This does not seem to be a matter of assuming the watch to be of value at the time of the theft, but then learning later that it was in fact of no value. Instead, this seems to be the contemporary assess-ment made by Singleton. Of course, Singleton might have been wrong in assuming the watch to be of no value. But this is, for pre-sent purposes, irrelevant. Singleton thought he was stealing a watch of no value.

A watch might well be of little market value, but of great use value under the circumstances, as in the case of a sip of water to an extremely thirsty person. But this does not seem to characterize Singleton's situation, objectively or by Singleton's own subjective judgment. Singleton was, on his worldview, motivated to try to reach some accommodation with his girlfriend, Cathy, and was frustrated in this by a lack of transportation. The victim's watch does not, frankly, seem terribly relevant. If time were of the essence in ren-dezvousing with Cathy, it is not entirely clear why one would want to delay one's progress to the extent required to murder and dispose of a nun, or, for that matter, how murdering a nun was likely to favor-ably impress a reasonable girlfriend.

Of course, it may well be that Singleton simply tended to respond to frustration in ways that did not promote either his short-term or long-term interests, and that even selfish but sensible risk-benefit assessments were at such times unlikely to inform Singleton's behav-ior. This is, however, precisely the point. We should simply admit that Singleton's mental world is apparently not easy for us to grasp or relate to, and that there may be much about it that we do not understand, even before we begin to ask what causes influenced his basic personality.

If this point needs further elaboration, consider Singleton's disposition of the nearly valueless watch. We may assume that either through murdering the nun or through the sheer passage of time, Singleton at some point ceased to be distracted by whatever frustrations were at work at the time of the murder. At some point, we would imagine, a nearly valueless watch would also be recognized as incriminating evidence. We would, if placed in Singleton's position, be inclined to doubt whether the value of retaining the watch was worth the rather obvious risk.

Singleton, however, apparently did not at any point reflect along these lines. It is conceivable that he appreciated, at least to some degree, the risk of retaining a valueless watch linking him to a murder, but that he drew some important psychic value from retaining the watch. This would of course be a matter of pure speculation. Perhaps Singleton looked on the watch as a token of an encounter with an at least initially friendly, apparently concerned individual. Perhaps the watch was a reminder of his superior physical strength or the ability to exercise his will to obtain a result. But even if one of these explanations actually described Singleton's state of mind, our point still stands. Singleton's retaining the watch, beyond the episode of the murder itself, is a decision to which we cannot really relate. We may eventually decide that Singleton is more evil, or more given to extreme, impulsive reactions to frustration than most of us. We may or may not wish to blame him, in whole or in part. But Singleton's mental world is, in crucial respects, simply not like our own.

Let us consider as well a detail from the case of the murderer Robert Alton Harris. Harris was the primary perpetrator of the murder of two teenagers. It is impossible to concisely and accurately convey the apparent sheer depravity of the two murders. But then, it is similarly impossible to convey the depravity of the life circumstances under which Harris was, in only the loosest, most metaphorical sense, raised. We shall attempt neither task. Instead, we will draw a single unusual inference from a detail of the killings that is, for some, most graphically indicative of moral monstrousness.

Robert Alton Harris, accompanied by his brother, had decided to obtain by theft a getaway car for use in a planned bank robbery. Harris chose a car occupied by two teenage boys eating hamburgers, forced the boys to drive to a secluded spot, and then brutally murdered both boys. Having left the murder scene in the stolen car, Harris was, within fifteen minutes, laughing and joking about the murders. Harris then finished the lunch begun by his victims by eating the remainder of their hamburgers.[7]

This appalling detail of the murders, while obviously not, by itself, an act of great legal moment, equally obviously bears on our assessment of the moral psychology of Robert Alton Harris. Finishing one's victims' uneaten lunch strikes us as, under the circumstances, horrifyingly evil. The incident reflects backward in time, distinctly unfavorably, on our assessment of Harris's general state of mind at the time of murdering the two teenage boys.

It is possible to undertake the heroically difficult task of inquiring into whether anything in the circumstances of Harris's life could be fairly and reasonably taken to mitigate, or even erase, Harris's moral responsibility for the two murders. Our point, however, is again far less ambitious. It is merely that we should not pretend that we understand Harris in all jurisprudentially relevant respects.

We should thus admit that whatever moral horror we feel for the act of finishing the victims' lunch, we also find the act literally incomprehensible. We cannot imagine ourselves doing it. We do not really see how anyone could. But Harris did. There is thus a gap between what Harris did and what we can explain. There is a gulf of incomprehension between our lives and his. No amount of empathy, identification, role playing, or the directed flow of imagination can close that gap. Certainly no social scientist, brain physiologist, or brilliant novelist can close the gap for us.

This, again, is not to conclude that Robert Alton Harris and Cornelius Singleton did not bear moral responsibility for their criminal acts. We should merely set some limits on our willingness to stigmatize what we cannot fathom. We do not precisely know, for all relevant judicial purposes, what it is like to be Harris or Singleton. Similarly, we do not precisely know what it is like to grow up under the bleak, grinding, occasionally horrifying circumstances of the most deprived.

This is not a counsel of agnosticism or despair. If we could, in the end, not even tentatively assess the effects of their circumstances on the most deprived, we could also never conclude that there is a case in which they did not genuinely and properly bear moral responsibility. We could not show the most desperate to ever bear moral responsibility, or the opposite. Issues of criminal moral responsibility in such cases would then be settled by presumption, or by which party was saddled with the burden of proof.

But we can, given our best, most careful, most dispassionate efforts, often intelligently assess issues of the criminal moral responsibility or blameworthiness of even the most deprived. As we undertake those tasks, however, let us not fill in the gaps in our knowledge by simply assuming that their circumstances, their opportunities, their mental maps, and the obstacles they face are, with some modification, pretty much like ours.

This point is clearest in cases where the incomprehensibility or the alienness of the defendant's act brings us up short. But we should recognize the validity of the point even when we feel sure we understand the defendant's motivation. We may, for example, find perfectly comprehensible why a starving person would steal a loaf of bread, or illegally beg, or why a homeless person might break into an abandoned building on an exceptionally cold night. We shall devote the following chapter to such cases on the assumption that the defendants in those cases can be legally responsible for those acts, for which we shall then consider a legal defense of necessity.

The error to avoid in such cases, if we think that we can easily understand why a desperate person would undertake just those desperate acts, is what might be called false identification. Most of us think we can imagine what it is like to be extremely cold or extremely hungry. We can then imagine seizing the perhaps single available means of redress, whether legal or illegal. But our ability to attempt this exercise does not mean that we genuinely understand what it is like to be chronically, desperately hungry, or chronically, desperately without legal shelter.

This is not simply a matter of our limited personal observations. If so, a middle-class person who affected the clothing, habits, and lifestyle of a homeless person, perhaps for a newspaper story, only to return on schedule to a middle-class existence, would be able to tell us literally everything we needed to know about homelessness. But this is of course impossible. No thoughtful person would claim that a cosmetic treatment, reversible or even irreversible, can allow a mature adult to truly and accurately grasp what it is like to be a member of another racial group, however illuminating the experience would otherwise be. Those who made it through college with low discretionary incomes for months or years at a time should, on reflection, admit that such an experience does not allow them to say that they have experienced what it means to be without resources and genuinely, chronically poor.

Even if we happen to assume, therefore, that breaking into a building, if necessary to obtain shelter, is a comprehensible act, we should not take, generally, the further and more ambitious logical step. We should not assume that we understand, for all relevant legal purposes, what it is like to be desperate, let alone chronically desperate, or to have been born into desperate circumstances. To the extent that

even great literature suggests that we can truly overcome this barrier, and have done so through literary genius, such literature again has
a falsely conservatizing effect in suggesting that severe deprivation is
no worse than we happen, from our middle-class perspectives, to
imagine it to be.

In particular, while it may be incorrect to assume that all those
subjected to the most dismal life circumstances cannot reasonably be
held morally responsible, it is also wrong to infer universal moral
responsibility from the welcome examples of actual success in overcoming harsh social conditions in socially approved ways. It is possible for flowers to grow in the most apparently barren soil.
Undoubtedly, most members of even the most deprived societal
groups are generally law-abiding. By analogy, some alcoholics and
drug addicts are capable of dramatic behavioral changes, with or
without treatment. But these facts do not themselves resolve the
important questions of moral responsibility. Certainly the ability to
adapt to or cope with genuine unfreedom does not show that one is
free. Persons who overcome extreme poverty and deprivation
through diligent effort may come to bear responsibility only through
their heroism, special help, saintliness, or luck, and it would be
unreasonable to demand such extraordinary capacities of everyone
as the minimal legal standard.

Our standards for responsibility must be reasonable in their
expectations and demands. It is tempting for any number of reasons,
including a mistaken understanding of the dignity and infinite value
of all persons, to generally hold the most deprived morally responsible, with only the standard, narrow legal exceptions. This is ultimately disrespectful of and harmful to the most deprived. The logic
of responsibility bars such an approach, however advantageous or
satisfying it might be on other grounds.

To see this, it is only necessary to think by analogy about the
nature and effects of literal, physical barriers with which people may

be confronted. Consider, then, an athletic high jump event. Depending on the height of the bar, the percentage of those clearing the established obstacle can be anywhere from zero to one hundred. Let us suppose that the bar has been set such that 70 percent of the contestants have been able to clear the height, while 30 percent have failed. Suppose further that all the contestants appear similar physically or at least that any differences seem random in their effects, that they have similar training histories, and that they have jumped under similar conditions. How would we think of the minority who failed to clear the height?

One possible perspective would be that those who failed deserved, for one reason or another, to fail. Perhaps they earlier faced a choice between self-indulgence and the discipline of additional training, and freely chose the former. But in any individual case, and certainly as an overall explanation, we would normally expect such responsibility-based explanations to play only a limited role. Even among self-selected athletic contestants, we would normally expect a multitude of factors to influence the outcome for which the individual contestant cannot reasonably be praised or blamed. Most obviously, individual effort cannot compensate for differences in access to training facilities or sheer individual physiological limits on one's high jumping ability.

In short, that an obstacle can be overcome by some or many apparently similarly situated people does not mean that failure to overcome that obstacle is, even in a nonmoral sense, blameworthy, or the responsibility of those who fail. Nor, in the world with which we are familiar, do those who fail to meet established legal expectations tend to have much control over what heights they will be legally expected to clear. The bar is set for them. Crucially, the bar can be insurmountable for them despite their reasonable efforts at all relevant times, and despite the fact that many others are able, heroically or as a matter of casual, almost effortless routine, to clear the same height.

It is possible to encounter a defendant who appears, as far as the available evidence shows, to have led a life of severe deprivation, and who similarly appears to have lacked all relevant control, freedom, and knowledge, but who nonetheless acted with responsibility in committing the charged offense, as we could appreciate only if a better understanding of the defendant's history and circumstances were available. We thus cannot rule out the occurrence of "false negatives" in matters of responsibility. There will, however, be similar "false negative" cases associated with any recognized legal excuse, including insanity. Some persons found legally insane may actually not be such. We accept some "false negatives" because we want to minimize the injustice of "false positives." There seems no sound reason to flatly ignore extreme deprivation unless we believe that the percentage of such "false negatives," in which courts let a genuinely responsible party off the hook, will be especially high. But feigning the adverse effects of long-term severe deprivation does not seem much easier than feigning insanity.

There is also the problem of setting a reasonably accurate but reasonably ascertainable boundary line for judicial purposes. How much of what sorts of freedom, control, and knowledge must exist, in one combination or another, for a sufficient level of responsibility to obtain? Precision is impossible in such determinations. The courts can err in imposing moral responsibility where persons in apparently similar circumstances avoid criminal acts, and the courts may also commit the opposite error. But again, unless we have reason to believe that a disproportionate number of cases will be "false negative" cases, it is obviously worth setting some reasonable legal standard, even given some arbitrariness in practice.

To refuse to set any standard is to commit the far more serious moral error of pretending that a substantial and reasonably identifiable group of severely deprived persons does not exist, and on that basis, inflicting undeserved punishment. When a court mistakenly holds a victim of severe deprivation to not be responsible, it is erring in favor of someone with whom few of us would care to trade places. Mistakenly finding someone to not bear responsibility for their acts does not in the slightest imply that such a person should simply be returned to the community with a license to commit antisocial acts. In any event, to refuse to recognize the possibility of nonresponsibility due to severe deprivation is to fail to recognize the moral importance of reforming the conditions of social life so as to increase the percentage of persons who can correctly be considered fully morally responsible.

To accommodate an obvious objection, we will superficially complicate our high jump metaphor. Most potential defendants can, on any given, specified occasion, refrain from violating any relevant legal rule. Such persons can, as it were, clear the bar on any single specified occasion. This includes victims of the most severe deprivation. Doesn't this show by analogy their moral responsibility? Such an inference, however, does not follow.

Not being responsible for one's otherwise criminal act does not mean that one must inevitably commit that act on every available occasion. That one is capable of once clearing a particular height, or of doing so a limited number of times per day, does not mean that one also has the ability to spend all day successfully clearing the height on every occasion. A person may not bear moral responsibility for an act even though she could, at least on that particular occasion, have done otherwise. A person may have the ability to refrain from a crime on some or any specified single occasion, while genuinely lacking the ability to refrain from that or a similar kind of act on all occasions over a period of years, if confined in particular social circumstances. Conceivably, one might not bear moral responsibility for one's addiction-induced behavior, yet be capable on some or any specified single occasion of not acting in accordance with one's addiction. The strength and peremptoriness of an addiction may vary over time, for example.

Similarly, within the narrow class of recognized legal excuses, the courts may find someone not responsible due to insanity, without implying that the insane defendant had inevitably to commit any crime, let alone the particular crime in question. Outside of the criminal context, the courts might, for example, hold an industrial worker morally responsible for failing to remove her fingers from a piece of machinery on some single distinctive occasion specified in advance, but not hold her morally responsible for her own injury if she is called upon to thus remove her fingers hundreds or thousands of times per day, day in and day out, where her injury involves no special occasion. Again, in such repetitive movement injury cases, the courts may find the plaintiff not responsible for her own injury without implying that the particular accident, or any accident at all, was truly inevitable.

Such inferences may well be disturbing to middle-class sensibilities. But too often, our willingness to impute responsibility to the most deprived is based, falsely, on a mental image of ourselves suddenly placed in a bleakly oppressive neighborhood, but while we retain our own current values, skills, knowledge, and experiences intact. Most middle-class persons, if involuntarily parachuted into an area of grim, concentrated poverty and limited opportunity, would feel no immediate attraction to violate familiar behavioral norms. This is, however, hardly the issue. Unfortunately, this unreflective sensibility is translated into judicial policy.

A certain amount of progress can be made by asking what reasonably could have been legally required of us, had we been subjected to the overall life circumstances visited on a particular defendant. But this inquiry, however useful in encouraging some limited empathy, eventually breaks down. Some middle class persons may give themselves the benefit of the doubt as to how they would have acted. Some may suggest that it is merely uninformatively true that if they had been subjected to exactly the circumstances, background, influences, and burdens of a given criminal defendant, they of course would have acted similarly. Others may rightly point out a serious problem in the logic of identity: To the extent that I am placed precisely in the complete relevant circumstances of another, it makes little sense to think of me as the person I was, as opposed to the person whose conduct I set out to evaluate, and the initial comparison becomes blurred.

One way around this problem of identity is to think not in terms of virtually becoming another person, but in terms of a proportion. We may start by wondering whether we could ourselves reasonably be held morally responsible for violating a particular norm. But we must also imagine that the ratio of constraints to resources we face is the same ratio of constraints to resources faced by any person to whom we propose to impute moral blame. Thus, we may continue to think of ourselves in many respects as we actually are, but we must then imagine ourselves facing unprecedentedly daunting obstacles to our continuous adherence to legal norms.

The main problem with these arguments is psychological. In most historical contexts, it has been both accurate and progressive for judicial systems to think in terms of equality of moral responsibility among persons. Persons are created equal in their moral status. But it is neither accurate nor progressive to infer, based on the absolute value and dignity of all persons, that even those facing the greatest barriers and with the fewest resources, through no fault of their own, bear moral responsibility for their acts equal to that borne by the privileged. To return to the athletic analogy, it is simply wrong to argue that if all competitors are in other relevant respects equal, competitors who must high jump six feet are just as responsible for failing to clear that height as those who must clear only a three-foot barrier.

It is possible, of course, to object that this whole line of reasoning, suitably developed, can be generalized to show that no one really bears moral responsibility. We often trace adult behaviors to early childhood environment within the middle class. For all we know, even the behavior of the most privileged persons is somehow caused. Can't the logic of exculpating some of the most deprived be extended universally, thereby undermining the whole point of moral responsibility?

Again, it is hardly the intent of this chapter to show that any conception of genuine moral responsibility is viable, beyond briefly suggesting below the unattractiveness of broadly supposing otherwise. We have set aside the broader issue of the viability of responsibility in a world apparently ruled by causal determinism and inherent quantum randomness. As we have said, it may be that all behavior is somehow caused by some combination of one's history, circumstances, and physical law. If so, we could hardly deny responsibility in the case of the most deprived, but not other persons, on the grounds that the behavior of the most deprived persons was somehow caused. At a less abstract level, useful and plausible distinctions can be drawn.

Admittedly, no one, regardless of economic class position, is in control of everything that may crucially affect her ability to comply with legal norms. We do not freely invent ourselves. We do not endow ourselves with our initial resources and constraints. But it does not follow that the idea of moral responsibility must completely unravel, or that if we absolve some of the most deprived of responsibility, we should equally absolve those whose crimes may have somehow stemmed from wealth and advantage. Until it can be shown that moral responsibility in its traditional legal and moral sense is incoherent or nonexistent, we can point to dramatic relevant differences between the unchosen environments of the most privileged and of the most deprived.

For example, the unchosen environment of the privileged is, almost by definition, an environment rich in opportunities, alternatives, and resources. One's legal environment tends to be responsive, accommodating, and forgiving. Knowledge of all sorts relevant to choice is at one's disposal. With privilege, ordinarily, comes some special power to control. These elements constitute nothing less than the material requisites of moral responsibility itself. The unchosen environment of the most deprived is, again almost by definition, rather less bountiful in the relevant sorts of opportunities, alternatives, and resources. Rather than accommodation, the most deprived are likely to encounter environmental indifference or threat. The unchosen environment of the rich is thus typically not relevantly stunting or constraining in the way characteristic of that of the poor. Thus, absolving at least some of the most deprived, while generally holding responsible those exposed to more favorable circumstances, is defensible.

Let us illustrate the point by referring to one of the best known among privileged criminals, the distinguished liberal arts professor James Moriarty. We may take as unimpeachable Holmes' description of Moriarty:

> His career has been an extraordinary one. He is a man of good birth and excellent education, endowed by nature with a phenomenal mathematical faculty. At the age of twenty-one he wrote a treatise upon the binomial theorem, which has had a European vogue. On the strength of it he won the mathematical chair at one of our smaller universities, and had, to all appearances, a most brilliant career before him. But the man had hereditary tendencies of the most diabolical kind. A criminal strain ran in his blood, which, instead of being modified, was increased and rendered infinitely more dangerous by his extraordinary mental powers . . . . He is the Napoleon of crime, Watson. He is the organizer of half that is evil and nearly all that is undetected in this great city. He is a genius, a philosopher, an abstract thinker. He has a brain of the first order.[8]

We need not take issue either with Holmes's general belief in hereditary criminal traits or genetic predispositions to crime, or his imputation of such qualities to Professor Moriarty in particular. Nor need we deny that Holmes's concern is in great measure for the sheer social dangerousness of Moriarty, or that a person can be extremely dangerous without bearing any moral responsibility for his actions. But Professor Moriarty is not merely dangerous in the way that an armed, nonresponsible lunatic might be. Despite whatever "tendencies" Moriarty may have inherited, we need not read Holmes as concluding that Moriarty was inevitably destined by his blood to a life of crime.

Moriarty, after all, was a professor. Professors, generally, have tangible or intangible resources and significant freedom as to the social dimensions of their lives. In most relevant respects, they understand and enjoy broad ranges of eligible options. Crucially, they know and appreciate that these options are available. Typically, nothing insurmountable stands, or even appears to stand, between them and a morally or legally conventional existence. The same simply cannot be said, invariably, of the desperate and the most deprived.

Appellate judges have not commonly found it appropriate to discuss the relationship between severe deprivation and criminal responsibility, at least in any systematic, general way. There are certainly exceptions. In a cocaine distribution conspiracy case raising a "private entrapment" issue, Judge Richard Posner wrote, for example, that

> All crime is a yielding to temptation, the temptation to obtain whatever gains, pecuniary or nonpecuniary, the crime offers. The temptation is a cause of the crime but not a cause that exonerates the tempted from criminal liability if he yields, just as poverty is not a defense to larceny. Cause and responsibility are not synonyms.[9]

While Posner's conclusion is thus that causation and responsibility are distinct, he could have made his point just as clearly by arguing that even though all crimes are somehow caused, causation does not preclude responsibility. A crucial cause of one's criminal act may be one's yielding to temptation. With Posner's assumption that poverty does not legally excuse, there need be no quarrel. Poverty, on some definitions, is compatible with the possibility of having, and knowing that one has, a reasonably wide range of viable life options available, hence a substantial measure of freedom, knowledge, and control. "Poverty," therefore, in the sense of at least current low income and wealth, need not be taken to be synonymous with the sorts of horrific circumstances with which we have been concerned above.

Judge David Bazelon, on the other hand, is widely associated with a substantially different approach. Bazelon wrote in a robbery and assault case that

> It may well be that we simply lack the resources—to say nothing of the understanding—that would be required if those who stole to feed their addiction were removed from the criminal process on the ground that they are not responsible for their actions. But if this is so, we should recognize the fact, and not rationalize our treatment of narcotics addicts on the false premise that their crimes are the result of a wrongful exercise of free will. It is to me intolerable that persons already crippled by an almost hopeless cycle of poverty, ignorance, and drugs should be further burdened by the moral stigma of guilt, not because they are blameworthy, but merely because we cannot afford to treat them as if they are not.[10]

We may in some cases want to hold an addict responsible even for crimes flowing inevitably from the addiction. Such defendants may in a sense not be morally responsible for the crime itself, if driven by the addiction, but moral responsibility for the crime may reasonably attach in cases in which the underlying addiction itself is blameworthy. Conceivably, a person could freely and knowingly risk or even seek addiction, appreciating that this choice could well lead to future powerlessness in the face of an addiction-driven need to commit crime. Bazelon's argument thus works best where we build in something like our approach taken above to the elements of responsibility.

In general, the courts are reluctant to consider any sort of material or social deprivation as undermining responsibility. Once the criminal defendant is assumed to be sane, the material and social circumstances of the defendant's life are generally thought irrelevant to the issue of guilt or innocence. On the other hand, if a sane defendant who has been convicted in a capital murder case has suffered extraordinary abuse or deprivation, then courts believe that they must consider such matters as possible mitigating circumstances, perhaps whether such deprivation bears any causal relation to the crime or not. Crucially, this consideration occurs only at the sentencing phase of the trial, after guilt has already been determined.

It may fairly be asked why such matters as severe deprivation are relevant only when an already convicted murder defendant faces the death penalty. No doubt the death penalty is qualitatively different. But the courts' logic in admitting evidence on such matters seems to be that social circumstances can reduce culpability or at least engender appropriate judicial sympathy. This logic would seem to transcend capital sentencing cases. Generally, the federal courts ignore the defendant's socioeconomic status in sentencing. This rule is thought to be neutral and impartial, akin to rules prohibiting discrimination in sentencing on the basis of the defendant's political beliefs. There is no obviously satisfactory explanation for the courts' apparent inconsistency in this regard. It may be simply that we are more reluctant to tolerate judicial hypocrisy and illogic when that illogic involves condemning a defendant to death.

Thus far, however, courts have been willing to consider what might logically constitute a complete defense, but only at the sentencing phase of the trial, after the jury has already determined, on what amounts to incomplete evidence, that the defendant bears responsibility for and is guilty of the charged offense. A jury might thus determine the defendant to be criminally guilty, based on the evidence actually admitted. But based on what the jury has only now heard at the sentencing phase of the trial, the jury may now, too late, come to believe that the defendant really cannot properly bear sufficient responsibility so as to be liable for the charged criminal offense. The jury might then prefer some alternative, less stigmatizing disposition, such as mere confinement, treatment, or isolation. As the law now stands, this possibility is not accommodated.

Let us also consider, hypothetically, a murder defendant who does not face the death penalty, but instead may be subject to a life sentence, along with a punitive fine to be paid from any future prison earnings. If the defendant in such circumstances can show reduced culpability, in that his criminal acts are clearly causally related to a severely disadvantaged background, the case for admitting such evidence in a noncapital case would seem strong, despite the legal system's current line drawing.

But there remains the deeper problem in the logic of the courts' procedure in such matters. Common sense and the commonly accepted logic of responsibility suggest that even in the case of sane defendants not acting with any currently recognized legal excuse, a defendant's moral culpability may be reduced or eliminated to the extent that the crime flows from a constrictive or horrific background, the effects of which the defendant could not reasonably be expected to escape. In some cases the defendant's background may carry the logical power to absolve him of responsibility.

The broader problem is inadvertently illustrated by the Supreme Court's quotation, in *Eddings v. Oklahoma*, of the logic of the underlying state appellate court opinion. The defendant Eddings, charged with a capital murder allegedly committed at age sixteen, claimed that he suffered from "severe psychological and emotional disorders, and that the killing was in actuality an inevitable product of the way he was raised."[11] The Oklahoma court granted the existence of a personality disorder, but did not otherwise address the defendant's claim that his history, or the disorder itself, made the crime inevitable. Instead, the Oklahoma court concluded simply that the defendant "knew the difference between right and wrong at the time he pulled the trigger, and that is the test of criminal responsibility in this State."

The Oklahoma court did not deny that the defense's claim of inevitability had been proven. Actually, claims that any specific single crime was inevitable are generally implausible. Instead, the court left itself in the position of holding that even if the defendant's act was indeed inevitably dictated by hostile external forces beyond his control, the defendant could still be convicted as long as he knew right from wrong at the time of the act.

But a mere cognitive grasp of right and wrong does not exhaust what is logically required for responsibility. Suppose that instead of being, as we assumed, inevitably driven by his earlier environment and personality disorder, the defendant had been forced to commit the murder under stark overwhelming physical duress, such that he had no real choice in the matter. Presumably the defendant would still have known the wrongness of killing at the time of his coerced act, but the Oklahoma court would not convict such a defendant. Why then does knowledge of the wrongness of killing somehow establish responsibility for some sorts of nonculpably inevitable acts, but not others? Isn't some degree of freedom and control generally also relevant to responsibility, unless the absence of freedom and control is itself culpable? Again, while the Supreme Court in *Eddings* reversed the exclusion of the evidence of family history, personality disorder, and so forth, it did so only as a matter of possible mitigating evidence regarding sentencing. The Court denied the relevance of such evidence to issues of guilt. Whether the defendant really was responsible regarding the charged offenses is, of course, not our concern. It is difficult, however, to escape the broader conclusion that the courts systematically mishandle and inconsistently apply the idea of criminal responsibility, according to the logic of the concept itself.

Let us assume that the case has been made that contemporary judicial doctrines and practices regarding responsibility are, in crucial respects, inconsistent or logically unjustified. It is no doubt still tempting to respond by suggesting that legal illogic should be tolerated if bringing the law into accord with logic would be socially dangerous or otherwise less attractive, from a practical standpoint, than the legal status quo.

There are costs and disadvantages in recognizing the judiciary's tendency to punish those not logically subject to punishment. Costs must be paid if we are to have more than merely random success in distinguishing those who do and do not bear moral responsibility for their actions, based on the kind of severe deprivation we have discussed above. We should admit that, as in the case of insanity or other defenses, there may be cases in which a defendant is found not to bear criminal responsibility due to severe deprivation, where the defendant would have committed the same act even if he had enjoyed privileged social circumstances. Severe deprivation may thus play no real causal role in crimes committed by the most deprived. This problem, however, obtains with regard to all defenses. The judicial options to manage the problem range all the way from expensive individualized inquiry to deciding such matters based solely on the defendant's residential nine digit zip code. We can thus alter the degree to which each trial may attempt to probe the psyche and biography of the defendant. The minimum goal, after all, is not to decide issues of moral responsibility correctly in all cases, but to significantly improve on the current pattern of universal judicial denial that extreme deprivation can ever preclude responsibility.

A deeper challenge to our approach, however, argues on utilitarian grounds for reducing or abolishing judicial efforts to accurately separate the responsible and the nonresponsible. It is plausibly argued, for example, that legally treating some persons as though they were morally responsible, even if they were not actually responsible, may have good general payoffs in terms of increased rule compliance, and might even lead those persons and others to actually begin to bear responsibility. One might make a parallel argument against the insanity defense. In general, a policy of treating people as though they were genuinely legally responsible may, as a behavioral conditioning device, have all sorts of possible positive and negative consequences.

If we compare the value of legal regimes with varying degrees of emphasis on moral responsibility, it is important to first note that properly holding persons morally responsible need not involve any element of judicial malice, cruelty, or vindictiveness. The potential gains from abolishing a logically sound nonvengeful judicial regime of moral responsibility may thus be limited. In the right circumstances, holding someone morally responsible may be a deserved compliment, rather than an expression of frustration or vengeance.

There is of course a natural uneasiness with deciding cases on the basis of any admitted legal fiction. Our ability to judicially abandon moral responsibility might even be questioned. It is not entirely clear that we could, given our culture and deeply held folk psychology, really give up the basic elements of the idea of moral responsibility. On the other hand, some form of denial of moral responsibility seems increasingly common among contemporary philosophers, and it is certainly possible to argue that at least a sharply diminished role for moral responsibility is a viable social possibility.

One possible approach to take, if one is sufficiently benevolent and self-effacing, would be to credit other people with responsibility for their good acts, but to not morally blame them for their bad acts. One might finish the pattern by accepting no genuine moral credit for one's own good acts, while morally blaming oneself for one's bad acts. Whether this pattern of attitudes is common, or is becoming more common, is largely an empirical question. Its stability as a pattern over the long term seems doubtful. In the meantime, this pattern of attitudes is itself morally ambiguous. The pattern seems on the one hand self-critical and well motivated. But the overall pattern is also logically groundless, in some respects elitist, and ultimately condescending. If one never deserves real credit, it is unclear why a range of other people do.

At a deeper level, we might begin to wonder whether the idea of objective morality itself, in familiar senses, can logically survive the rejection of the basic, familiar idea of moral responsibility. Objectivity in morals is a complex idea. For our purposes, however, we may think of objectivity as aspiring to truth or realism, as opposed to being admittedly concocted or invented to serve some independently chosen interest or purpose. It may be, perhaps, that moral responsibility is actually an illusion, but one that we cannot, for biological reasons, abandon. If we thought this to be so, we might decide to temper the severity of the legal consequences we inflict on the most deprived defendants. The poor, we might decide, have already suffered, and much of this extraordinary suffering might have been due to legal rules or public policies many of us view as unjust. The poor have, on such a view, already made at least a "down payment" on any criminal sentence, and the legal system itself may have been a causal influence on the extraordinary suffering and even the crime itself. But if objective morality itself is on no firmer logical grounds than moral responsibility, why, morally, should we be generous to the most deprived, beyond what mere prudence dictates? If objective morality itself came to be seen as an illusion, why not amuse ourselves at the expense of the least powerful and those who cannot retaliate? It could hardly be objectively immoral to do so. If objective morality is an illusion, it is not objectively unfair to simply overlook or excuse any role the legal system may have in causing any crime.

Among those who doubt that anyone is morally responsible for their criminal acts, there is some uncertainty as to the practical implications of this view. If we discover that there really is no such thing as moral responsibility, free will, blameworthiness, or praiseworthiness as traditionally conceived, that of course could not logically be deeply embarrassing for us. That sort of deep embarrassment would logically be gone as well. There is certainly no reason for an organic machine to be embarrassed that it is only a machine, even if it once thought otherwise. On the other hand, there would equally be no indignity or deep embarrassment if we chose to pretend, contrary to fact, that moral responsibility existed. If we are just organic machines, we need never be genuinely embarrassed by anything, including our lack of moral responsibility or our decision to pretend that all or some of us can bear moral responsibility. It seems possible as well to admit our incapacity for moral responsibility, and then still strongly prefer a democratic as opposed to an elitist legal regime. We could do so on the grounds of the former's assumed greater likelihood of ruling in accordance with our basic tastes and preferences as organic machines, though of course not on grounds referring to any human dignity linked with moral responsibility.

It has been suggested that denying all moral responsibility need not mean that the legal system must logically abandon all reliance on objective morality itself. There is reasonable concern, however, that without familiar ideas of moral responsibility and related notions, we are, in all relevant respects, really nothing more than complex, social, cognizing, sentient, organic robots. Galen Strawson has argued that in the absence of free will and moral responsibility, "no one in fact acts morally rightly." Strawson grants that

> there does remain a sense in which we can be said to do the objectively morally right thing just in performing certain types of acts in certain circumstances, even though we are not in fact free agents. But in the end, it is only, and exactly, the sense in which a robot, or at least an ordinarily sentient being that has no conception of moral right or wrong, can do the morally right thing.[12]

The denial of moral responsibility and moral agency may indeed leave us as organic robots, and undermine the objectivity of morals. But there is certainly nothing to stop anyone who denies moral responsibility from also preferring, arbitrarily or otherwise, that the legal system operate, say, to maximize overall public happiness. Such a person could apply the terms "just" and "unjust," "fair" and "unfair," or "right and wrong" consistently with this understanding. Perhaps there could be some prudential, self-interested reason for each of us to seek to maximize public happiness, rather than directly pursuing more selfish courses.

In any event, it is widely suspected that the moral world that would survive the death of moral responsibility would strike us now, with our current attitudes, as variously debilitating, dreary, merely animalistic, two-dimensional, mechanical, cold, shallow, or terrifying, involving a reduction of the quality of our human relationships, or simply involving a great loss of value. While some sorts of emotion and attachment could survive the death of moral responsibility, there would likely be, from our current perspective, a certain manipulativeness or hollowness to such attachments. Abandoning, as opposed to reforming, the use of the familiar basic notion of moral responsibility thus seems unattractive.

If only as a matter of making a virtue out of literal necessity, some are tempted to overstate the favorable and understate the unfavorable consequences for the most deprived and for disadvantaged persons generally of abandoning moral responsibility in its standard senses. Consider, again, the possible linkage between moral responsibility and morality itself, in any objectively binding sense. What clear reason can be given to suppose that the disproportionate power of the powerful can be systematically reduced without offering any purportedly objective moral reason to justify this process? Being systematically and severely deprived means that one has relatively little with which to bargain or threaten. Those in such a position must rely, at least in part, on objectively good reasons. The most deprived may report their suffering and call for change, but this is unlikely to have much impact if it amounts only to a mere report or expression of or about their circumstances, state of mind, or bare preferences. Where is the logical incumbency in our acting on such reports and expressions, in the absence of any objective weight?

In a world without moral responsibility and any objective morality, the rich, certainly, could not claim to morally deserve their greater wealth. Nor could the better-off continue to enlist the idea of moral objectivity, abusively, as a weapon with which to injure the poor and the disenfranchised. So far, so good. But equally, the desperate could not offer any objective moral claim to any redistribution of wealth in their favor. Perhaps, some prudential, merely group-based, ultimately arbitrary arguments could be advanced in any direction. But that state of affairs would tend, presumably, merely to reinforce the existing general inequality of resources. It is far from clear that persons of good will should welcome the dilution of the idea of the objective moral dignity of all persons, including the poor and the oppressed. None of this is to suggest that merely offering objectively good reasons for social change must produce social change. But if it is indeed the powerful that are to be called on to sacrifice, objectively good reasons to do so seem necessary.

Even if it serves no other purpose, however, the movement to hold no one morally responsible should inspire us to revise current judicial practices to accord with our best understandings of moral responsibility, moral value, and the dignity of the choosing person. When the criminal justice system properly holds persons responsible for their acts, it recognizes in the defendant the dignity that is in all persons, and we should avoid a system of trial, sentencing, and incarceration that in any respect denies that dignity.

It has been argued, however, that recognizing even some of the most deprived as not responsible is both socially dangerous and disrespectful to those so classified. But fear for the public order from an expanded class of persons recognized as really not bearing moral responsibility is misplaced. There is no logical need to immediately return such persons to the community, to judicially confine them for only trivial periods of time, or to release them upon completion of some ineffective therapeutic regime if they have committed dangerously harmful acts. It is hardly vindictive or improper to confine otherwise criminal offenders who pose unreasonable dangers to their neighbors for as long as they pose such a danger. Dangerously harmful acts may justify confinement or treatment, even if not blame. There is a broad range of possible dispositions of such offenders that neither falsely impute moral responsibility to the offender, nor jeopardize the basic safety of the community.

The claim that expanding the category of those not morally responsible for their otherwise criminal acts would undermine the dignity or potential dignity of those actors is in a sense more interesting, but even more clearly wrong. It may be thought that a finding of nonresponsibility for an act might lead to judicially imposed therapy or some sort of allegedly rehabilitative treatment for the offender. With compelled therapy, or rehabilitation, there is the risk of sheer manipulation of the offender. Whether traditional sorts of therapy or rehabilitation are likely to be effective over the long term for the most severely deprived is also a significant issue.

It is therefore crucial to recognize the difference between therapy or rehabilitation on the one hand, and the development of the conditions and capacity for properly being held morally responsible on the other. Our interest is in the latter. Rehabilitation aims at changing the behavior of the offender from antisocial to prosocial, or from being inclined to commit criminal acts to not being inclined to commit such acts. In short, rehabilitation aims at making the offender morally good, or inclined to perform good acts. One might or might not then be morally responsible for those good acts. This, however, is not at all what we mean by promoting the conditions under which it would be reasonable to hold the offender morally responsible.

Creating the conditions in which it becomes reasonable to hold persons morally responsible does not in the slightest imply that those persons will be morally good, or will obey the law. By itself, bearing moral responsibility does not at all imply that one will do the "responsible" thing. Bearing responsibility in a moral sense generally includes the capacity to choose to act wrongly as well as rightly.

What is the point, then, of the criminal justice system's participating in a broad societal effort to enhance persons' capacities to be held morally responsible for their actions? The first point has to do with practicality. It is possible that we, as a society, have a better idea of how to promote the conditions for reasonably being held responsible than we do of how to rehabilitate offenders, or to make them good. That is, we may know more about morally enfranchising persons than about how to make them good. This enfranchisement, or the promotion of the conditions of responsibility, would require a politically awkward egalitarian redistribution of opportunities. Enhanced public efforts to provide pre- and postnatal nutrition, genuine public and personal physical safety, preschooling and daycare, education, socially meaningful employment opportunities, and housing might well be required. Promoting a person's capacity to bear moral responsibility is largely a matter of relevant sorts of freedom, control, and knowledge on the part of the actor. It is certainly possible that we know how to enhance these sorts of things, regardless of cost, better than we know how to make an offender good. It is also possible that providing the basic conditions for moral responsibility may actually tend to improve people's behavior, but we need not insist on this point.

More crucial, however, is the enormous dignitary value of the capacity to act, for good or ill, in such a way as to bear moral responsibility. There is, of course, a societal interest in self-protection that may require confinement of offenders and perhaps some program akin to rehabilitation. But there is also an extremely strong moral interest in transforming social circumstances so that potentially responsible actors will come to bear full responsibility. In this process, the law and the state can play an important role. We do not enhance the dignity of those denied the capacity for morally responsible choice by pretending, through the judicial system, that they do bear such responsibility. It is backwards to imagine that a judicial system promotes dignity by falsely ascribing moral responsibility to any group of persons. The first step in developing or enhancing the dignity of criminal defendants is for the legal system to realistically categorize such persons, without engaging in self-serving metaphysical flattery of defendants in ways that obscure and trivialize the real effects of long periods of undeserved severe deprivation.

It may seem to violate the dignity of a person to place that person, without consent, into circumstances under which the person for the first time is now reasonably subject to valid ascriptions of responsibility. Some persons who currently cannot properly be held morally responsible for their acts doubtless may prefer to remain that way. By hypothesis, however, that is not a responsible or autonomous choice. There is much to be said for the dignitary value of transforming a person's social circumstances so as to develop for the first time the person's capacity for responsibility, even if coercion is involved. The coercion involved is the coercion of terminating an unnecessary and clearly undignified wardship. It is coercion for the sake of creating autonomy. This is not a matter of, in the name of freedom, telling people how to behave. The abuse of such coercion is radically limited by the purpose of its exercise: to promote the social conditions of responsibility, which include freedom, knowledge, and control. However much a few might want to resist this kind of social maturation, it is hardly a serious restriction on their freedom and dignity to provide the conditions of freedom and responsibility to such persons for the first time. In fact the presumably rare desire to remain nonresponsible may simply reflect the coercive, stultifying restrictiveness of one's familiar environment.

Now, depending on one's moral schema, one may already ascribe dignity, and perhaps infinite moral value, to every human being, whether they bear responsibility for their acts or not. But this returns us to a deep philosophical issue. At some risk of paradox, it seems plausible that even if all human beings are of infinite moral value, whether they are currently capable of moral responsibility or not, there are reasons, based in theories of human development, human fulfillment, or Kantian morality, to see substantial if not infinite moral value in leading persons from a condition of nonresponsibility to one of moral responsibility. To do this the state and the legal system would have to act affirmatively to promote knowledge, freedom, and control on the part of those currently most deprived thereof.

This is not a matter of the totalitarian manipulation of otherwise free persons' minds. Leading persons to autonomy does not involve such manipulation even if we already attach infinite moral value to those who are not yet capable of bearing moral responsibility. It is not a matter even of instructing the poor on moral right and wrong.

It is not a matter of paternalistically treating adults as though they were children. Rather, it is a matter of arranging the most basic elements of persons' broad social and economic circumstances so as to promote the development of the capacity for real moral agency itself.

The crucial idea is that full moral agency and the capacity for bearing moral responsibility are not always self-generating within humans, and are not utterly independent of social and economic circumstances. The capacity for moral responsibility has general material and social conditions. Doubtless, once the capacity for moral responsibility is developed, it may persist despite extremely adverse social circumstances. Heroism, for example, may take the form of a continued capacity for moral agency despite the imposition of severe burdens on that capacity.

Further, it is morally and logically arbitrary to find great moral value in one's own capacity for bearing moral responsibility, but to see no such value in that of other human beings. If developing one's own capacity for such responsibility is morally important, so it is as well in the case of others, even beyond one's own group or one's neighbors, who through no fault of their own lack such capacity for moral responsibility.

It may be technically true that no one can directly cause anyone else to have, for the first time, the capacity to bear moral responsibility. Actually, it is hardly clear why such a thing is impossible. But this technical question is in any event of no great consequence. What a society ought to do is provide the necessary material and social conditions for the development and exercise of the capacity for moral responsibility.

Certainly, this is not the only relevant moral duty a society might bear. It is, for example, also incumbent on societies to protect and perhaps enhance the capacity for moral responsibility that has already been developed within the citizenry. There may be interesting moral conflicts in this regard. A government might, for example, face a trade-off between protecting and enhancing the capacity for responsibility in group A, and promoting the initial or minimal attainment of such capacity within group B. It is not our task here to argue at length that in such cases of conflict, group B should generally receive a higher priority than group A. But there is an obvious and strong moral case for such a presumption.

This is not to suggest that providing the necessary material and social conditions for the capacity for responsibility must always override any other moral and political goals. But there is a clear egalitarian logic to such a social policy, and an admittedly less clear, but still reasonable, intuition that initially sparking a full moral life into a human being outranks merely enhancing such a capacity in others. Regardless, providing the social prerequisites to responsibility will certainly morally trump a number of other concerns, including slightly greater disposable incomes for the rest of the population.

What is particularly interesting and unusual about this general approach is the possibility of combining egalitarianism and a concern for freedom with a crucial emphasis on expanding moral responsibility. It is, after all, commonly thought to be an important weakness of contemporary liberal and progressive thinking that they seem to awkwardly underemphasize the very idea of responsibility in individual action. But there is really nothing inherent in progressive thought that disables it from cogently discussing issues of responsibility in the criminal law and elsewhere.

This chapter illustrates the crucial lines of reciprocal support between egalitarian redistribution of resources and the value of responsibility. Any approach that offers to coherently combine emphases on equality, freedom, and moral responsibility should be attractive to legal reformers. The attractiveness of this approach is further enhanced if we can largely bypass political controversies over the historical causes of the current circumstances of the most deprived. Leading persons from a condition of not generally bearing responsibility for their acts to a condition in which they do can largely be accomplished without resolving in detail a number of such disputed questions. We can make substantial progress, for example, in developing and enhancing a broader capacity for moral responsibility without raising the controversial question of the extent to which any current incapacity for moral responsibility was ever intended by the powerful or by the broader society. Among the payoffs for largely bypassing such questions is a sharper focus on the enormous moral value of changing social circumstances so as to broaden the possession of the capacity for moral and legal responsibility.

This is not to suggest that contemporary advocates of equality have generally ignored all issues of responsibility. In a largely "negative" way, the idea of responsibility is central to modern egalitarianism. After all, one criticism of discrimination seems roughly to be that it is unfair and unreasonable to stigmatize or even merely burden persons on the basis of qualities or events over which they had no appropriate degree of control.

With such an approach, we have no dispute. One of the aims of this chapter, however, is to transcend such concern for identifying cases in which persons can or cannot be held responsible and then judicially treating them differently on that basis. Instead, we have also emphasized the importance of increasing the percentage of persons to whom responsibility can be fairly imputed. In the meantime, the hypocrisy involved in holding responsible those who do not meet the criteria for responsibility should be candidly recognized.

Desperation and Necessity:

Les Miserables on Trial

Let us suppose that the argument of the previous chapter was utterly mistaken. Even the most severely deprived persons could then be said to typically bear moral responsibility for their criminal acts. Of course, standard defenses, such as self-defense and insanity, might still be relevant. A severely deprived person, though morally responsible in all relevant respects, could still be legally excused or justified in exerting reasonable and necessary force to discourage a stranger's unprovoked, life-threatening attack. And a severely deprived person who happens to meet whatever standard the law sets for the defense of insanity would, presumably, on that ground be absolved of legal responsibility. But in general, even the broadest, most chronic and profound deprivation would leave the offender open to legal blame.

Defenders of the criminal justice system would emphasize that the law does not completely ignore severe deprivation among criminal defendants. In some cases, the defendant's severe deprivation is judged not to completely absolve that defendant of criminal responsibility, but to somehow constitute a "mitigating circumstance" for consideration during sentencing. If, on some theory, the deprivation is thought legally relevant, though not sufficient to undermine the defendant's responsibility, the criminal justice system translates a somehow mitigating deprivation into a less severe sentence than might otherwise be imposed.

It is not surprising that the courts would consider severe deprivation in this limited way. Judicially considering such deprivation as a possible mitigating circumstance is useful for system maintenance and legitimation. A criminal justice system that always imposed an unabated criminal sentence on those whose chances of avoiding criminality were obviously limited would pay an unnecessary price in reduced public support and in the morale of criminal justice system actors. Some jurors, certainly, would tend to feel a potentially disruptive sympathy for criminal defendants whose circumstances were both criminogenic and unpleasant in the extreme.

Allowing for the possibility of reduced sentences in such cases thus reduces any uneasiness felt by those operating the criminal justice system and by the broader public. The legitimacy and stability of the criminal justice system is enhanced, and two major costs are avoided. First, the public avoids the cost of alternatively treating or possibly even simply releasing obviously dangerous criminal defendants, on grounds of absence of moral responsibility. Such defendants are instead simply incarcerated in traditional fashion, thus protecting the public, although for a period of time shortened in some proportion to the degree of mitigation found.

Second, society avoids the question of whether it should pay the public cost of reducing the number of persons raised in circumstances of severe deprivation. Sympathy might otherwise lead to a social attack on such severe criminogenic circumstances. But the promptings of sympathy are themselves "mitigated" through our judicially mitigated response to the criminal defendant. Currently, the defendant's severe deprivation may be "factored in" or "credited" toward his criminal justice "account." Whether such crediting is mandatory or discretionary is of secondary importance. More crucial is that the criminal justice system may, at least on its own accounting, partially balance the scales of fortune. This limited redressive process is largely intuitive and subconscious. But at some level, for example, a certain number of stray bullets in one's housing project is judicially thought to suggest a certain reduction in one's criminal sentence, as though the defendant were, loosely, receiving some credit for time served. Roughly as the criminal defendant's pretrial jail time might be credited against the prison sentence eventually imposed, so the Dantesque character of one's life circumstances are turned to one's minimal advantage as a mitigating factor in sentencing.

The problem, however, is that while the consciences of one's sentencers may thus be cleared, the criminal justice system may, having thus partially restored some overall moral equilibrium for the defendant, then rest content. Our collective inclination toward benevolence is not unlimited. If we have even partially restored the defendant's overall moral balance sheet through benevolently reduced sentencing, this may dull our appetite for the more crucial task of reducing the extent to which persons grow up under conditions of severe deprivation. Thus we have only a reduced inclination to undertake the latter, far more morally and politically significant task.

Once the criminal justice system determines the severely deprived defendant to bear legal responsibility, the system then proceeds to the defendant's guilt or innocence. Severe deprivation is considered, if at all, only as a mitigating factor with regard to sentencing. This chapter argues, however, that as a matter of fairness and the criminal justice system's own officially established logic, severe deprivation should in some cases be taken far more seriously. In particular, severe deprivation may be relevant as the court considers possible complete legal defenses to the criminal charge.

The law has, in one fashion or another, long recognized the possibility of complete defenses such as self-defense, duress, and necessity. Such defenses need not deny that the defendant bears moral responsibility for the act in question. These defenses are sometimes thought to legally excuse otherwise wrongful conduct, or to actually justify the defendant's conduct under the circumstances. We shall devote most of our attention to the logically proper scope and limits of the defense of necessity.

In particular, we shall seek to understand and apply the defense of necessity in the cases of persons who can fairly be said to suffer from severe current deprivation in certain basic practical respects. Specifically, we will focus on the defense of necessity in the cases of those who are without money and who illegally beg, those who are without shelter and who illegally obtain shelter, and those who are without food and who illegally obtain food.

We will discuss the precise legal elements, or the constituent parts, of the necessity defense below. But for now, even a rough, intuitive idea of necessity will suffice. Imagine a person who, through no fault of her own, finds herself in desperate jeopardy of life or basic health, such that her jeopardy can, apparently, be relieved only by committing some relatively minor criminal act, as by stealing a loaf of bread or sleeping in an abandoned building. For now, this simple image of necessity will do.

Not all thefts of food or shelter will attract our sympathy. Not all such crimes fall within the proper scope of a necessity defense. But one cannot dismiss a necessity defense in such cases on the grounds that if the argument of the preceding chapter has failed, such defendants must be presumed morally responsible for their conduct. Even if true, that is beside the point. This chapter does not simply reargue the previous chapter in the context of particular kinds of pathetic cases. The necessity defense can, at least arguably, be raised by persons who admit their general moral responsibility regarding the charged criminal conduct. Certainly at least some jurisprudes would see no inconsistency in a defendant's accepting moral responsibility for an act, yet pleading the defense of necessity. On some theories, one who legitimately relies on a necessity defense might have made a wonderfully informed deliberative choice, even if under necessitous circumstances.

Admittedly, the elements of the necessity defense are not utterly separate from those of general criminal responsibility. Issues of knowledge, freedom, control, power, and capacity are clearly implicated by both. But since necessity is at least sometimes thought compatible with general moral responsibility, we will treat the necessity defense separately. There may well be an overlap between the most severely deprived and those who might plausibly raise a necessity defense in the case of direct, bare survival-oriented crimes. But it is still possible that a valid necessity defense could be raised by someone who fairly meets the minimum genuine requirements for moral responsibility. Perhaps the best-known case arguably falling into this category is that of the notorious nineteenth-century bread thief Jean Valjean.

Let us consider the circumstances of Monsieur Valjean, as depicted by Victor Hugo. Valjean's theft has been described as "dull-witted."[1] His sentence of five years hard labor has been referred to as "excessive."[2] But is the basic problem either dull-wittedness or an excessive sentence? The Valjean bread theft case has, as a precedent, been fertile.[3] But it is not clear that it deserves to be.

Of course, no brief description of a life, even by a master of the order of Victor Hugo, can be anything other than the crudest sketch. There may be inherent biases in such sketches. And certainly, no mere excerpt from such a sketch can do anything but further drain the sketch of any relation to reality. But consider, nonetheless, a portion of Hugo's account of Valjean:

> In the pruning season he earned eighteen sous a day, after that he hired out as a reaper, a workman, teamster, or laborer. He did whatever he could find to do. His sister worked also, but what could she do with seven little children? It was a sad group, gradually held tighter and tighter in the grip of misery. One very severe winter, Jean had no work, the family had no bread. Literally, no bread and seven children.[4]

Now, we may assume that despite the harsh circumstances of his life in general to that point, Valjean bore the capacity for full moral responsibility for his acts. Certainly his later successes as an inventor, entrepreneur, and mayor would suggest that his childhood had not permanently narrowed his capacities unduly. Valjean himself would apparently not claim that the theft was involuntary or not a willed act.

Nor, interestingly, would Valjean himself wish to claim even a defense of necessity, despite his initial bitterness toward society for its treatment of him, and toward what he sees as an unfairly severe sentence. Valjean sees the economic and legal system as at least as much at fault as he is, but he certainly does not deny a share of the moral and legal guilt for himself. In particular, Valjean denies, at least in retrospect, the literal necessity of the theft. He could have waited. Perhaps the children could have waited. Perhaps the bread would have been given to him. Perhaps work would have turned up in time. It takes a substantial period of time for even a small child to die of starvation. Valjean does not assume that some other adult would have stepped forward to provide for the children, or that their lack of food was to any degree his fault. But the unavailability, or the evident unavailability, of realistic alternative courses of action to avoid or reduce the looming severe harm is an element of the necessity defense, and Valjean doubts that this element was really present.

We shall consider below the difficult question of what sorts of more or less evident and viable alternatives must be available in order for the defense of necessity to properly be barred. In the meantime, we must insist that Valjean is at this point second-guessing himself, after being removed from the necessitous circumstances. In prison, he can be of no further use to those seven dependent children. That Valjean now regrets the theft is understandable, even if the elements of a necessity defense were actually present at the time of the offense.

Thus we cannot grant Valjean the sole prerogative of pronouncing judgment on a possible necessity defense, even in his own case. Valjean certainly deserves the first and most extensive word on his own circumstances. But this Valjean is not yet the saintly, or even the merely more insightful Jean Valjean. Just as criminal defendants may seek unreasonably to evade responsibility, so, with opposed unreasonableness, they may for various reasons react to their own acts with undue severity and authoritarian punitiveness. Criminal defendants are not invariably the best judges of their legal status. Some defendants who might avail themselves of a legitimate necessity defense do not fully appreciate its logic, standards, and application in their own case, for cognitive or emotional reasons. Thus we cannot say, even from Hugo's brilliant account, whether Valjean could properly have been acquitted through a necessity defense, even if a properly contoured such defense had been available, and had been properly explained to Valjean.

We should also note a particular biasing effect built into great characters in great literature. Such characters cannot be considered great unless they hold our interest. But what holds our interest in a character is richness, complexity, subtle shading, growth, and development. A character that is flat, dim, uncomprehending, or undeveloped, as in the case of Champmathieu in *Les Miserables*, tends to exert only a lesser hold on us. But this means that the great characters in literature will tend, as requisites of greatness, to display a capacity for moral responsibility, resistance to even overwhelmingly adverse circumstances, and nuanced, subtle, resourceful, alterable responses to challenges, even if tragically unsuccessful, for reasons within or beyond their control.

Jean Valjean is a great and memorable literary character. But we should not expect great and memorable literary characters to illustrate the absence of the basic elements of responsibility, or even, to an admittedly much lesser degree, the requisites of the defense of necessity. This is as true of the tragic and criminal characters of Sophocles, Shakespeare, Dostoevsky, and even Kafka as it is of those of Victor Hugo. Characters who can most plausibly be said to lack the requisites of moral responsibility, or even to fall victim to necessity without fault, tend not to hold our interest and thus do not lend themselves cogently to artistic exposition of the absence of criminal responsibility.

Bearing this systematic biasing factor in mind, however, there is still much to learn from Valjean and other literary characters presented in *Les Miserables* regarding the defense of necessity in the case of direct, bare survival-oriented crimes. The character of Valjean in turn inspired Emile Zola's depiction of Nanet in Zola's *Work*.[5] In *Work*, the six-year-old Nanet steals a loaf of bread to feed himself and his famished older sister, against the background of a disastrous labor strike, as a result of which "hunger was impelling wretches hither and thither." The gendarme who apprehends Nanet gives him "a shake in order to frighten him. `You'll go to gaol, you know,' he said. `Why did you steal that loaf, eh?' But the little fellow was not put out. He answered clearly in his flute-like voice: `I've had nothing to eat since yesterday, nor my sister either.'"

As it happens, Nanet is at this point rescued by the personal, idiosyncratic intervention of a benevolent stranger, as Valjean himself is at a later point in *Les Miserables*. Without a trial, there can be no necessity defense. We shall see below that avoiding trial is not an unmixed blessing for the desperate. We shall also see at length that the currently recognized scope of the necessity defense is narrow. The necessity defense is invoked successfully more commonly in circumstances of natural disaster or social class-neutral emergency than in the circumstances of the desperately poor, or of those whom the society and economy have returned to something approaching a Hobbesian state of nature.

If it turns out that the necessity defense is indeed currently unduly crabbed given its own underlying logic, and plainly not class-neutral in its application, it would seem to be in the interests of the desperately necessitous to expose, if not alter, that state of affairs. This exposure, however, of the arbitrary narrowness and systematic bias of the established necessity defense requires trials, appeals, and published opinions in the most appropriate cases. But no such opinions are written if those cases presenting the best vehicles for exposing the illogic and inequity of the law are dismissed systematically prior to trial or appeal.

In this regard, the motivations of those who prevent the trial and appeal from occurring are irrelevant. Even if the police, prosecutors, or courts are motivated by boredom, pity, or generosity, their actions ultimately inhibit proper testing of the scope of the necessity defense, to the long-term detriment of the most desperate among us. Particularly with regard to illegal begging and illegal seeking of shelter by the homeless, systematic pity tends to prevent cogent challenge to the established scope of the necessity defense and perpetuates the cycle of desperation, offense, official pity, and discharge from the judicial system. The possibility of using a successful challenge to the current limitations on the necessity defense to exert pressure for a more constructive response to class-based desperation is thereby lost.

Thus for our purposes, the basic problem faced by the hungry is not, as Mr. Limbkins presumes in *Oliver Twist*,[6] that those who assertively presume to do something about their hunger will eventually be hanged, but that they have been denied a useful judicial precedent invoking the necessity defense, widely applicable to the genuinely desperate, that could provide an incentive for the legal and political system to constructively address the straitened circumstances of the desperate.

As might be imagined, the problem of prohibited acts of survival-oriented desperation occurs more commonly in the contexts of illegal attempts to find shelter and illegal begging than in the context of thefts of food. But actual bread theft cases do occasionally occur. Among the few reported appellate food theft cases addressing a possible necessity defense is the Depression-Era case of *State v. Moe*,[7] decided by the Supreme Court of the State of Washington. Again without fully addressing the complexities of the law of necessity, let us briefly consider the circumstances of *Moe*.

In this case, the defendants were convicted of grand larceny, in that the value of the food stolen was shown to exceed the statutory minimum of twenty-five dollars. Apparently, a large group of unemployed persons had, on the afternoon of September 3, 1932, gathered together and marched to a Red Cross relief center in the city of Anacortes, demanding an increase in their relief allocation of flour. Thus some sort of allowance or flour ration was already in place. But the supreme court's opinion does not offer any particulars; thus we do not know the extent or frequency of the flour distribution, its adequacy in relation to need, or the realistic possibility of any increased distribution of flour. The opinion gives us very little grounds for characterizing the conduct of the flour distributors as heroically generous, perfunctory, negligent, or malicious. Thus it is equally impossible to assess fully the moral standing of the food thieves, who may correspondingly have been motivated by a sense of patent, readily correctable injustice, or by an irresponsible, if understandable, desire to selfishly improve their position relative to equally or more desperate unemployed persons, where the food donors and distributors had acted with saintly self-sacrifice.

We should be suspicious of any judicial opinion addressing the necessity defense that does not allow us to intelligently assess the moral status of the defendants. Of course, no judicial opinion can present a full and accurate picture of the degree of desperation present, any more than can even a great novel. But we need not ask the courts to determine and concisely articulate the state of mind of the defendants with penetrating accuracy and subtlety. The applicability of the necessity defense need not depend on courts' accomplishing the impossible. Courts constantly make reasonably accurate assessments of defendants' states of mind, in civil and criminal cases, at reasonable cost. Degrees of desperation can thus be assessed, based on the testimony and objective circumstance. Once assessed, the degree of desperation can enter into the court's consideration of the plea of necessity. That we cannot read the minds of Valjean, Nanet, or Iver Moe with infallibility should not bar their pleas of necessity, any more than it should bar their claims and defenses in other criminal contexts or in tort or breach of contract cases.

As *Moe* reports, the unemployed group was told by the ranking Red Cross official that it was impossible to comply with their demand for an increased flour allowance. Again, the court apparently saw no relevance either in the accuracy of this assertion or, if accurate, the cause and possible alterability of this condition. At this point, several members of the unemployed group announced their general intention to resort to self-help, and the group left the Red

Cross site. A large group, variously estimated at from forty to seventy-five persons, proceeded to a privately owned local general store or grocery store. This group entered the store and, over the protests of the owner, seized food in disorderly fashion and left without making payment. At least one threat of physical violence against the store owner was made, after the owner had locked the store with him and the unemployed group inside, to induce the owner to then unlock the store. At least one defendant, however, apparently took no food, and threatened or encouraged no one. The supreme court's opinion refers to the scene inside the store as a riot, but the opinion does not provide much feel for the degree of disorder, violence, or absence of group self-control.

At trial, the defendants offered to prove what the supreme court refers to as "conditions of poverty and want" at the relevant time among the local unemployed, in order to show lack of premeditation, motive, and most importantly for our purposes, "justification" for their acts. The supreme court opinion reports that in the course of his argument to the jury, one of the defendants argued to the following effect:

> The groceries were taken, of course, but remember this, there is a higher law that says that a person holds his responsibility to himself first. There is a law of self-preservation, and how can you expect a man to go against the most fundamental urges—the most prominent is the quest for food. Even the cave man in days gone by must have food.[8]

Finally, it must be noted that the *Moe* case was not without political overtones. In closing argument to the jury, the prosecutor referred to the defendants as radicals and communists. The supreme court determined that this did not taint the verdict, as the jury had been immediately instructed to disregard the remark, and the defendants had during jury voir dire referred to themselves as members of militant labor organizations, with two of their number reporting membership in the Communist Party.

The supreme court's response to the defendants' asserted necessity defense is notable largely for its brevity. The essence of its reasoning was simply that "[e]conomic necessity has never been accepted as a defense to a criminal charge. The reason is that, were it ever countenanced, it would leave to the individual the right to take the law into his own hands."[9] While the court cited no relevant legal authority, we may assume the accuracy of its statement of the law.

There is much to say about the court's analysis and application of the law of necessity, and we shall have relevant points to make throughout the remainder of the chapter. But even at this point, it is important to notice the inadequacy of the court's opinion, and to speculate a bit as to why this case in particular, on its facts, might have found its way into the reported appellate cases.

First, the court's reasoning is unsatisfactory in the most basic sense. It cannot literally account on its own terms for the established case law of necessity. The court's view is simply that the individual cannot be granted a right to take the law into the individual's own hands. In most contexts this is a useful maxim, but its logic obviously extends beyond cases of purely "economic" necessity. While it is a useful corrective against vigilantism, it may also stand in some tension with legitimate self-defense or the defense of others. More important, and more directly, such reasoning casts as much doubt on noneconomic necessity defenses as on economic necessity defenses. Yet the law clearly recognizes the legitimacy of the necessity defense in some noneconomic contexts.

Consider, for example, the case of a recreational hiker who through no fault of her own is caught alone in a remote area in the midst of an obviously life-threatening blizzard. She has no means of transportation or communication. Unless she quickly obtains shelter, she will, as she appreciates, die of exposure. But it is equally plain that the only realistically available source of shelter is an unoccupied but privately owned storage shed. The hiker does not know the owner of the shed, and cannot seek and obtain permission to use the shed. Perhaps entry into the shed can be accomplished only by damaging the door.

Let us assume that the hiker saves her own life in this fashion, and is otherwise liable for criminal trespass. Does she nevertheless have a viable defense of necessity? We may fairly assume that most courts would recognize a valid necessity defense in such cases. Let us then ask whether, under the logic of the *Moe* case, the hiker has taken the law into her own hands. Either she has, or she has not. But either answer poses problems for the court in *Moe*.

Let us suppose that the hiker, no less than the hungry defendants in *Moe*, has taken the law into her own hands. This, then, corresponds to the *Moe* court's stated reason for rejecting the necessity defense. The *Moe* court would thus be similarly bound to reject the hiker's defense of necessity as well. But this is contrary to what most courts would do, given the hiker's circumstances. The defense of necessity has at least some minimal scope, and it is typically applied in such cases. The *Moe* court would then have to explain its departure from the standard result in such cases.

But perhaps the *Moe* court would deny that the hiker has taken the law into her own hands. This line, however, is of little real help to the *Moe* court. It must be explained how the hungry defendants in *Moe* took the law into their own hands if the hiker did not. What is the relevant difference between them with respect, precisely, to taking the law into their own hands? We may have some idea as to what taking the law into one's own hands amounts to. There is a certain vagueness to the idea, however, and the court in *Moe* provides no useful guidance.

Plainly, there are interesting differences between the circumstances and actions of the hiker and those of the defendants in *Moe*.

We may assume that the hiker is not pressing a defense of "economic" necessity, in the sense of poverty- or class-related necessity, whereas the defendants in *Moe* are. But what does the economic or noneconomic nature of the alleged necessity have to do with whether the defendant is taking the law into the defendant's own hands? Even the hiker presumed to consciously violate what would normally be legally established property rights.

Certainly, the actions of the defendants in *Moe* were more threatening, alarming, and riskier for the persons of others than those of the hiker. We do not claim that such considerations are irrelevant to the validity of a necessity defense. But again, what does this obvious difference in the two cases have to do with whether either or both have taken the law into their own hands? Not all economic necessity cases will involve any personal threat to any property owner. Not all economic necessity cases involve a grievance against some person or institution. We are assuming that the hiker, in entering and perhaps breaking into the unoccupied storage shed, was committing an illegal act at her own initiative, apart from the defense of necessity. The acts of the defendants in *Moe* were, again apart from any possible necessity defense, also illegal. Why are the presumptively illegal acts of the hiker not an instance of taking the law into her own hands, in parallel with the presumptively illegal acts of the defendants in *Moe*?

No satisfactory answer seems available. We are left with only the sense that while the hiker and the defendants in *Moe* equally broke the law—either one has broken the law or one has not—the latter's violation of the law was more serious, or more socially threatening, both to individual shop owners and to the established order. This, however, is not an obvious definition of "taking the law into one's own hands." The court is entitled to define terms as it wishes. But if by taking the law into one's own hands, the court refers to something like the commission of a relatively serious or institutionally threatening crime, it should say so.

And if this is indeed what the court in *Moe* means by "taking the law into one's own hands," it must face a further problem. The court plainly wants to treat all cases of economic necessity as invalid and as, to one degree or another, instances of taking the law into one's own hands. But common sense again suggests that some cases of economic necessity are not as dangerous or threatening, at least to the shop owner, as others.

Consider a hypothetical case of a starving, plainly unarmed small child who discreetly shoplifts an apple from a sidewalk display and then moves on, unnoticed by the shop owner, who was known by the child to be inside the store at the time. The child may not see her hunger as reflecting injustice. The court in *Moe* must evidently reject any claim of economic necessity in this or any other case. But can the court say, by way of explaining the idea of taking the law into one's own hands, that this was a particularly serious, threatening, or dangerous theft, at least to the individual shop owner? Was it any more threatening or dangerous than the conduct engaged in by the hiker?

One might say that a victim was at least vaguely present and potentially threatenable in *Moe*, but not in the hiker case. But can this distinction save the *Moe* court's reasoning? What if the facts are again altered? Suppose the starving child pilfers the apple from an unattended vending machine, in the presence of no human witnesses, but is caught on a remote security camera, or by a relentless latter-day Inspector Javert. The necessity defense in such a case would still be economically based, hence unacceptable to the *Moe* court, yet no personal threat could have been involved. Or what if the hiker happens upon the storage shed, but the owner is in fact within the shed, too ill to respond to the hiker? What if the hiker knows this? What if the owner does not know the hiker's intentions? Would the *Moe* court now deny the necessity defense to the hiker on the grounds that in posing some sort of unintended threat or risk to the owner, she has taken the law into her own hands?

Actually, we need not claim that the idea of taking the law into one's own hands is merely a question-begging label reflecting the court's independent reluctance to accept the defense of necessity in particular cases, or in all cases of economic necessity. The idea is still salvageable in a way that accords with the traditional case law, however ultimately indefensible that traditional case law may be.

We have seen that economic necessity cases need not involve any greater personal risk or threat to a property owner than cases of noneconomic necessity. But not all risks and threats are merely personal. Some acts threaten basic societal arrangements, institutions, and class structures. Such threats may be explicit or, more commonly, merely implicit. Such threats certainly need not be powerful. But they are recognizable, and the cases can be reasonably well sorted on this basis.

At least in a broad sense, economically based necessity claims, typically involving possible starvation, homelessness, and poverty, normally pose this sort of explicit or implicit threat to a society's class arrangements. The threat is, of course, typically not the ripeness or prospect of revolution, but the rightness or the mere possibility of some redistribution of wealth or property rights along class lines. The threat need not be intended or even recognized by the defendant; most commonly, it will not be.

There is, however, an "edge" to economically driven necessity defenses that is largely absent in the case of noneconomically driven necessity defenses. Our hiker case, for example, by itself carries no relevant class overtones, and lacks obvious class implications. Recreational hiking and camping are not typically engaged in by the wretched of the earth. Not even by implication does the hiker's trespass carry any obvious threat to the system of class structure, beyond the general implication that human life or health should take precedence, in this and similar cases, over the property rights with which those vital interests may conflict. In contrast, cases of economic necessity raise, if only by unintended implication, more threatening inferences. They may call into question the justice or utility of economic and property rights systems in which some persons are, through no fault of their own, reduced to desperate circumstances and left with few options.

If we assume, then, that the *Moe* court's reasoning was driven, at least unconsciously, by what we may refer to as system-maintenance interests, we must then ask why *Moe* is a published, reported appellate case. Why wasn't Iver Moe sent to the limbo of judicially unreported status? Doesn't publishing an opinion in *Moe* raise implicitly the possibility of broad, systemic change? Why not let the sleeping dog of economic necessity lie?

Consider again the facts of *Moe*, in contrast with those of Jean Valjean or Zola's Nanet. Consider in particular whether the otherwise potentially disturbing defense of economic necessity could, under the specific facts of *Moe*, be raised, briefly discussed, and rejected on appeal, with reasonable psychological comfort and plausibility. As reported, the facts in *Moe* are considerably less favorable to a necessity defense, all told, than those constructed by Hugo or Zola. Doubtless any behavior, by any person or group, evokes some sympathy and compassion if it is driven by hunger. But the contrasts between *Moe* and the circumstances depicted by Hugo and Zola are pronounced.

First, neither Iver Moe nor any of his fellow defendants is a street gamin of the sort romanticized by Hugo. Zola's Nanet is a pathetic six year old urchin. Admittedly, Valjean is twenty-five years old at the time of the bread theft. But we see that he is stealing the loaf largely to feed seven minor children. It may of course be replied that for all we know, Iver Moe and his fellow defendants may have been motivated largely by a desire to feed their children as well. This is a reasonable supposition. But the *Moe* opinion, it should be noted, is utterly silent on this point. If any small children are hungry in *Moe*, they make no appearance in the judicial opinion.

Let us contrast as well the matter of numbers and decorum. In *Moe*, a group of from forty to seventy-five persons, described as a riotous mob, descends on a single defenseless store owner, threatens him, and strips his shelves in the fashion of a plague of locusts. We must admit that neither Valjean nor Nanet does a better job of spreading the cost of their pilferage; in each case the loss is left concentrated, at least prior to any insurance claim, on a single, arbitrarily selected property owner.

It may well be that none of the store owners in these cases has enjoyed a supply monopoly or acted unjustly. And grocery store owners may be no more responsible for hunger or poverty than, say, hardware store owners, yet persons on the verge of starvation who wish to avoid robbery tend to focus their attention on stores that sell food rather than radial saws. The arbitrariness involved is undeniable. But there remain differences among the cases. A disorderly group of at least forty adults is simply more threatening than an unarmed six-year-old. A shop owner may feel victimized in both cases, but can reasonably fear for life or safety in only the first.

In addition, the degree of loss, insurance aside, is significantly different in the two kinds of cases. We know that some amount in excess of twenty-five dollars' worth of food was stolen in *Moe*. Without seeking to control for the effects of inflation or price differentials, we may fairly assume that nineteenth century loaves of bread typically sold for only a small fraction of that amount. There is thus a difference in the concentrated magnitude of the loss. Now, a street urchin may tend to steal food more frequently than an Iver Moe or, for that matter, a Jean Valjean. But there is no reason to suppose that street urchins as a class tend to single out particular bread sellers to the exclusion of others. Even if one particular street urchin concentrates his attention on a particular store, others may similarly concentrate on a different store, exempting the former. The store owner in *Moe*, however, may reasonably see himself as disproportionately burdened, at least if other local food store owners existed and were not targeted on this or any other occasion.

Let us consider a final difference among the cases. Again, the court in *Moe* is not as forthcoming as it might have been in this respect. But consider the role of what might be called third party hunger. We know that some charitable allowance was being made in *Moe*, that the eventual food thieves demanded more, and that this demand was officially rejected as impossible to fulfill. It is possible, reading the facts in a way least favorable to the defendants in *Moe*, that their demands and thefts were selfish, in that the defendants might have improved their position only at the expense of other poor, hungry, and unemployed persons.

This is not to suggest that the most illuminating way to analyze the problem of hunger is to pit one starving person against another in a zero-sum game and compare their degrees of self-restraint. Plainly, there is no reason any society should be organized in such a fashion that one person's subsistence must involuntary worsen the position of someone who is equally if not more desperate. But this may, for all we are told, have obtained in the *Moe* case. If so, the moral status of the defendants' acts in *Moe* would be correspondingly affected.

This would seem to contrast with the likely third party consequences in the cases of Valjean and even Nanet. We must admit that a harsh winter is likely to have adverse effects on persons other than Valjean and those dependent on him. Certainly, no coherent social system can feature universal theft, or the universal theft of bread from private shop owners. Most people cannot be stealing consumer goods most of the time. But it is difficult to argue that Valjean's theft, either by itself or in its likely social context, adversely affects persons who are no better off than Valjean.

Valjean's theft may well have prevented some other desperate person from either buying or being given that particular loaf. It could be that Valjean's theft tended, minimally, to increase the price of bread by some fraction, or even to provoke the closure of the shop in question, in ways adverse to the interests of the poor in general. But the problem is not a general shortage of bread, in the sense of an unmarketability or the physical unavailability of bread. Valjean's theft does not, in any concrete, significant way, worsen the short- or long-term circumstances of anyone else who is at least equally hungry.

Nanet's bread theft may be analyzed in similar terms. It seems clear from the setting depicted by Zola that bread theft has, even under the grim circumstances of the local strike, hardly reached epidemic proportions. The general local crime rate is, by our own current standards, apparently quite low. Bread producers and sellers do not seem demoralized. There do not seem to be any grounds for supposing that anyone else suffers even indirectly as a result of Nanet's theft. Again, this is in potential contrast with the circumstances of *Moe*.

This is not to suggest that the local shop owners are in fact untroubled by Nanet's theft. In the local post-strike environment, they fear the possibility of any isolated crime's inspiring other crimes, resulting ultimately in widespread disorder, riot, and violent class conflict. Even Nanet's pathetic theft is thus not devoid of possible systemic implications. It is not impossible that the actions of a group of radical trade unionists in Depression-era Washington might have inspired similar anxieties.

But it is the differences between the circumstances of *Moe* and those of Valjean and Nanet that best explain the court's willingness to briefly discuss, if only to dismiss, the economic necessity defense. We have seen the likely differences among the thefts on dimensions such as the helplessness of the beneficiary, numbers involved, personal threat level posed by the thief or thieves, disorderliness, magnitude of the thefts, and the differences in possible effects on third parties in at least equally desperate straits. And it must not be forgotten that the defendants in *Moe* were already receiving at least some charitable assistance, perhaps even the maximum assistance that was feasible under the circumstances.

Under the facts in *Moe*, even a court that is preoccupied with threats to established economic arrangements might see value in briefly discussing and rejecting an economic necessity defense. The defendants in *Moe* risked nothing by raising an economic necessity defense at trial and on appeal. But their facts and circumstances were, as we have seen, in various crucial respects simply less favorable and evocative than those of Valjean or Nanet. Nor do there seem to be any obvious respects in which the defendants in *Moe* present a more sympathetic case for a necessity defense than Valjean or Nanet.

The court in *Moe* was thus able to point to various relatively unattractive facts and circumstances in that particular case and, on that basis, to rule without psychological discomfort that the law disallows presenting the defendants' economic necessity defense to the jury for consideration. Under the relatively unappealing facts of *Moe*, no serious moral wrong seems involved in thus ruling against these particular defendants. One can certainly imagine a jury rejecting a necessity defense, if given the opportunity, under the facts of *Moe*. This result might well depend on factors such as venue, voir dire, and the use of peremptory challenges by the attorneys. But in general, jurors might consider a broad prohibition of all economic necessity defenses far more unjust in some cases than others.

As we have seen, however, the court in *Moe* did not attempt to craft some carefully tailored, narrow rule. *Moe* did not hold open the possibility of a contrary result in a case with significantly different facts. To paraphrase a great admirer of Zola, the writer Anatole France, the law in its majestic equality denies a necessity defense to riotous mobs and dewy-eyed starving waifs alike. The court in *Moe* thus claimed, in dicta, to bar a jury's consideration of an economic necessity defense in any and all cases, on even the most sympathetic possible facts.

The court in *Moe* may thus have viewed the case, consciously or unconsciously, as an almost ideal vehicle to stabilize and reaffirm established property institutions. The court could, by implication, legitimize nonthreatening, nonsystematically redistributive necessity defenses, as in our hiker example. At the same time, the court could reject an economic necessity defense in a relatively unsympathetic case and purport to place all possible economic necessity cases under the same absolute, exceptionless bar. The advantage, of course, is that it is easier to rule against, for example, the six-year-old Nanet's necessity defense if Nanet and his circumstances are neither before the court nor present in the minds of the readers of the *Moe* opinion.

It will not have escaped notice that food is not the only necessity, and that the theft of food is not the only possible direct physical survival-oriented crime. Begging, too, even for the sake of food, is illegal in surprisingly many jurisdictions. Less surprisingly, obvious strategies for obtaining shelter used by the homeless to ward off health threats, or out of sheer exhaustion, are often illegal as well. Let us consider in turn, then, the dimensions of illegal begging and illegal means of coping with one's homelessness, with an eye toward a possible necessity defense in such cases.

We must admit that there is something a bit odd about seeking to establish a legal defense of necessity to a criminal charge of begging for one's basic sustenance in otherwise appropriate cases. It is difficult to see such a defense, or the state of affairs underlying that defense, as the crowning achievement of civilized society. Subsistence begging should not be necessary in the first place. For those interested in genuinely constructive political change, a limited defense of necessity may seem unimportant or undesirable. At least a moment's consideration of the subject is, however, appropriate. After all, not being arrested for subsistence begging may, for understandable reasons, be preferable to the beggar. And if it matters to some of the least well-off among us, it should matter to those of us who are insulated from such circumstances.

Apparently, roughly half of the states and a large number of municipalities significantly restrict or flatly prohibit begging, at least on one's own behalf, as opposed to more organized charitable solicitation.[10] The reasons for restricting or prohibiting begging are obvious. Beggars often induce fear and anxiety in passersby. They are often unattractive, or unappealingly different. Their begging may result in financial proceeds beyond what is necessary for subsistence. They may devote the proceeds of their begging to drugs or alcohol. They may not even be genuinely needy. They may induce guilt or raise otherwise avoidable moral and political issues. They may induce crossing the street, or avoidance of eye contact. They may discourage shopping, and may amount to signs, if not actual causes, of local economic decay. In congested areas, they may be thought especially threatening. In some cases, they may be detectably mad. In some perhaps not easily predictable cases, they may be verbally abusive, hostile, or persistent.

On the other hand, those who reject the idea of a necessity defense in the case of food theft may recognize at least one reason to tolerate begging. Whatever else we say about a necessity defense, it should require that no plainly better alternative means of avoiding the threat be clearly available. And in some cases, a brief instance of begging, especially legal begging, will be such a preferable alternative, from the standpoint of the shop owner, or society in general, to the theft of food. Of course, the alternative of successfully begging for subsistence, legally or otherwise, may not always be practically available.

There would be no need for a necessity defense to the crime of begging if, as a matter of constitutional law, begging could not be substantially regulated by the criminal law. And there is certainly something to this possibility. Begging commonly involves speech in public places. Even a beggar's failure to literally speak or to use a written sign does not necessarily mean that the beggar is outside the scope of the free speech clause. A beggar may rattle or merely extend a tin cup. While not literal speech, that may amount to the sort of symbolic conduct that the Supreme Court has recognized as raising free speech issues. Wearing a black armband of protest, burning a draft card or a flag, or saluting the flag do not involve literal speech either, but they similarly raise free speech issues.

It seems clear enough that someone who publicly burns a draft card intends to convey a reasonably determinate opinion on some social issue. We may infer, for example, the draft card burner's distaste for a war or the draft as an institution, though we might of course be wrong in this inference. The draft card burner's point may be quite hazy or merely personal. But this is not the most obvious inference. Can we offer a parallel analysis, however, in the case of verbal or nonverbal subsistence begging?

For many, the pinch of necessity in general and acute hunger in particular may tend to constrict cognitive and motivational horizons. The concrete and the personal tend, under such circumstances, to displace the general and the abstract. Thus we may say that some beggars have, in the act of begging, no intention to convey any determinate idea regarding any broader social issue. Their message may be simply that they, in particular, are currently hungry, a condition that they, autobiographically, find unappealing. But it seems plausible that with some frequency, a broader, more general message is intended as well.

Thus in some cases, the beggar may intend, verbally or nonverbally, to raise broader themes associated with human suffering, human equality, human dignity, the virtue of charity, or even the demands of justice. These themes need not be the predominant element of the beggar's message. Nor need the beggar's speech touch on such exalted themes in order to invoke free speech protection. Rightly or wrongly, the Supreme Court has given substantial constitutional protection to speech that is intended to express only narrow and mercenary ideas. The Court has, for example, found significant constitutional protection for purely commercial speech, as in a proposal by a particular vendor to a sell a particular, nonideologically charged good to a particular buyer at a particular price. It is difficult to believe that the speech of beggars only rarely reaches a corresponding level of constitutional value.

In fact, if we set aside any broader political or social themes implicit in the speech of beggars, we may conclude that the beggar's speech falls within the protectable commercial speech pattern. Why may we not say that the beggar is proposing, at a minimum, a discrete commercial transaction, if not a commercial relationship? Commercial speech does not lose its protection merely because it is unpopular or unsuccessful. Of course, begging may differ from buying and selling in some respects. It might be said that the beggar's proposal is actually to be given some indeterminate sum of money in exchange for nothing. To this, two replies may be made.

First, it is difficult to believe that commercial speech is within the scope of the free speech clause when one party receives nearly nothing in the exchange, but not when the value received moves from being infinitesimally small to precisely zero. Presumably, a lost and found classified ad does not start out with no free speech protection, only to gain such protection as soon as the possibility of a small reward is mentioned. It is difficult to see why an offer to give away one's real property to a worthy charity would not be protected speech, if an offer to sell such property to a charity for a dollar is protected. In all these cases, of course, we are assuming the absence of fraud, deception, coercion, and other objectionable elements.

Second, most or all donations to beggars involve some form of benefit to the donor. This is so even if we unrealistically assume that begging involves absolutely no costs, including pride and dignitary costs, to the beggar. The donor in such cases may receive, or believe herself to be receiving, anything from euphoria to a clear conscience, a sense of magnanimous superiority, or an enhanced likelihood of reward post-mortem. Or one may be glad of the opportunity to impress one's companions. All these may extend beyond merely removing the psychological unpleasantness created by encountering the beggar in the first place. And the possibility that one might have donated truly selflessly, in the absence of these benefits, does not seem crucial to the free speech analysis.

Public begging, even if it involves action or conduct, seems deserving of some degree of free speech protection, and this is generally the line taken by the courts. Thus a complete prohibition of peaceful begging in public places, including broad public sidewalks in non-residential areas, has been struck down as insufficiently justified and as unduly restrictive of the free speech rights of beggars. On the other hand, the free speech rights of beggars have not prevailed in the already anxiety-provoking New York City subway system. "Aggressive" begging has been held prohibitable, in light of obvious practical concerns. And begging, along with solicitation of all kinds, has been held prohibitable on certain public beaches and related sidewalks.[11]

We may conclude that while begging deserves and receives some degree of free speech protection, begging is and will likely remain commonly illegal in many of the places in which it most naturally occurs. The governmental authority wishing to restrict begging may cite incompatible public interests and carefully craft the limitations on begging in accordance with those interests. Or a government may carefully avoid any public reference to begging, and instead restrict begging along with more institutional charitable solicitation, justifying the restriction solely by reference to the ills associated, under the circumstances, with solicitation in general.

The free speech clause thus does not do away with the need to consider a necessity defense in the case of genuinely survival-oriented begging. This is not to suggest that the courts have yet actually recognized any necessity defense in the case of even the most blameless subsistence begging. To recognize even a narrow defense of necessity for even the most clearly hapless beggar would, after all, amount to a damaging official admission of the insufficiency of public programs and private charity.

In fact, begging for one's survival, or that of one's dependents, runs up against something of a paradox. The more clearly innocent of fault the beggar is, the more desperate the beggar's circumstances, and the clearer it is that the beggar has no realistic alternative to begging, the greater the official embarrassment in recognizing a necessity defense. Thus the more clearly deserving the beggar is of a necessity defense, the less likely, all else being equal, the defense is to be recognized, in light of the greater official embarrassment in admitting the need for such a defense under such circumstances.

It is, after all, one thing to stigmatize and successfully prosecute a defendant whose criminal conduct can at least partially be traced to his own slothfulness, self-indulgence, or panicky overreaction. It is quite another to similarly stigmatize someone who has evidently suffered mightily, and has exhibited none of the above vices. As a society, we are not particularly troubled if those we rightly or wrongly deem "undeserving" fall through the safety net. To admit that the conscientious or the innocent may fall through the safety net as well is more troubling.

Thus the existence of the genuinely "deserving" subsistence beggar poses a distinctive problem for the judicial system. The courts might choose to recognize a narrow defense of necessity in such cases in order to avoid compounding the defendant's undeserved misfortune or mistreatment with a stigmatizing criminal conviction. Or the courts might choose to add judicial insult to social injury by pretending that all begging is essentially alike, and that beggars do not genuinely find themselves in necessitous circumstances. In practice, the law has generally chosen the latter, easier, if ultimately ignoble course.

Similarly unflattering observations might be made of the judicial system's disinclination to recognize any sort of necessity defense in food theft cases and in what might be called "housing theft" cases. Still, the sense admittedly lingers that there is something especially demeaning, unworthy, passive, and unprogressive about a legal defense for the act of public begging. The life of the poor would not be dramatically improved merely by a license to beg. Such a license by itself tends to validate underlying distributions of economic opportunity. All things considered, however, interest in a necessity defense for some acts of public begging is not entirely misplaced. Admittedly, a defense for necessitous begging would likely not pose the same sort of moral, ideological, and practical challenge to the basic distribution of wealth and property that might be posed by necessity defenses in the case of food or housing theft. Even a hard-to-obtain and quite narrow "license to steal," under limited circumstances, and with proper compensation to property owners, would be more likely to provoke alarm. Such a necessity defense would likely, however, also result in some pressure to change economic and welfare institutions, in constructive ways, so that the requirements of even a reasonable necessity defense could not be met. This would presumably mean providing greater realistic opportunities for obtaining minimal food and shelter than are now universally available.

But a "license to beg," obtained through judicial recognition of an appropriate necessity defense, does not sound quite as threatening as a legal permission to steal. If it is less threatening, it may for that reason be more likely to eventually be officially recognized. But can it equally lead to constructive economic change? One would guess not, though even a "license to beg," if that crudely oversimplified shorthand may be permitted, may exert some pressure for progressive change.

Consider, for example, that the legalization of begging does not eliminate its disturbing elements for pedestrians, shoppers, and merchants. Once it became clear that some sort of necessity defense protected some instances of begging, even where the beggar's free speech rights might not prevail, pressure to reach some sort of accommodation might arise. If begging were otherwise legally here to stay, enhanced incentives would arise to provide for realistic alternatives to begging or theft, thereby quite reasonably undermining any claim of necessity. Presumably, these alternatives would combine realistic availability with discreet invisibility to the broader public. Such realistic alternatives might be geographically concentrated, though widely accessible, or geographically dispersed. The trade-off for the broader public, presumably, would be enhanced efficiencies, reduced individual transaction costs, economies of scale, and a visible urban commercial landscape perceived as inviting and economically healthy, rather than disconcerting and distressed. Thus a necessity defense even for begging may have some limited potential for inspiring constructive institutional change. This constructive potential must, of course, be weighed against the risk that recognizing a necessity defense for some instances of begging will serve mainly to legitimize current economic relationships and to inhibit more significant systemic reform. This calculation cannot be done once and for all, or in the abstract.

Let us turn, then, to the related question of a necessity defense in the context of otherwise illegally obtained housing or shelter. In particular, we shall consider cases where such accommodations are allegedly necessary to preserve life or avoid serious threats to health, where no reasonable alternative housing arrangements are practically available, and where the defendant's desperation and lack of alternatives do not reflect the defendant's own fault. We will discuss this problem in the context of poverty-based homelessness, but the discussion may have some bearing on somewhat different kinds of cases, as in the case of a battered woman who is reduced by circumstances to the barest of options.

Estimates of the current scale of American homelessness vary, but no typical estimate is reassuring.[12] Commonly, persons are arrested, if not prosecuted, for what we have loosely called the theft of shelter or housing. Part of the looseness of this terminology reflects the fact that "theft of shelter" may take the form of temporary residence either in abandoned buildings or in public parks or other exposed areas not typically classified as housing stock of any sort. We intend to address such arrests, under theories such as trespass and curfew violation, beyond the narrow housing-oriented property rights violation suggested by the idea of "squatting."

The idea of a necessity defense in some such cases is of course complicated. Part of the underlying social problem consists of substantial mismatches between persons with given resources and capacities, and the size and costs of the legally and practically available housing stock. There is certainly no guarantee that minimally adequate housing will be available for persons with relatively low incomes. Cities have fewer single room occupancy facilities than formerly. There is, ultimately, a difference between desperate need and effective market demand.

But the problem of homelessness is obviously not reducible merely to a disproportion between the need for and the supply of cheap, legal housing. Municipalities sometimes fear, reasonably or unreasonably, that every step they take in accommodating the homeless will eventually be undermined by attracting an influx of the homeless from other jurisdictions. On the other hand, the homeless face the problem of a civic "race to the bottom." Once one city discourages the homeless from remaining, surrounding cities naturally fear an influx of homeless persons from that city. This fear exerts increased pressure on surrounding cities to follow suit by similarly discouraging the homeless. These fears are based not only on considerations of a limited local tax base, lack of state and federal aid, and fear of a need for increased expenditures, but also on the belief that the homeless tend in general to be problematically "different."

After all, the size of the contemporary homelessness problem is sometimes traced at least in part to earlier movements to deinstitutionalize the mentally ill. To the extent that mental illness and drug and alcohol abuse genuinely contribute to the problem of homelessness, homelessness itself is not reducible simply to a failure of housing markets to clear.

It is relevant to the defense of necessity in particular that some percentage of the homeless fall into these unfortunate categories. Undoubtedly most courts and jurors are not generally inclined to think of non-substance abuse related mental illness as the fault of the mentally ill. Thus in an appropriate case, a homeless defendant raising a necessity defense should certainly not necessarily lose on the grounds that she would not have been homeless, or would not have had to resort to illegal housing, but for her nonculpable mental illness.

On the other hand, it is easy to imagine courts and juries rejecting a necessity defense to an illegal housing charge if the defendant's homelessness or recourse to illegal housing is traceable to the defendant's assumed fault in abusing drugs or alcohol. And this is, to a degree, a matter of logic. We would rightly be unsympathetic to a necessity defense raised by a hiker who willfully assumed the risk of being stranded by deliberately venturing, without protection, into a dangerous storm. We would similarly be unsympathetic to the bread theft by Jean Valjean if we knew that he had been entrusted with money for bread but, knowing the circumstances, had frivolously and quite freely gambled the money away a block from the bread shop.

Certainly, in such cases there in a sense remain necessitous circumstances. The hiker and Jean Valjean are still in desperate straits.

But reasonable courts and jurors could well reply that the necessity in the case was culpably of the defendant's own making. At least some housing-based necessity defense cases may be like this. Even if a genuine necessity is thought to exist, the law might say that the necessity and the charged offense could well have been avoided by available reasonable prior choices by the defendant, even if other persons or institutions may bear some share of the blame as well.

Thus the defendant's homelessness, or criminal response to homelessness, may reflect in part the defendant's own assumedly voluntary substance abuse. Of course, if the defendant is an addict, we may not wish to blame the defendant for acts stemming from the addiction that are somehow involuntary or not reasonably within the defendant's current power to control. But courts may wish to trace those acts in turn back to an initial voluntary, perhaps blameworthy choice to take illegal drugs or to risk addiction or alcoholism. How appropriate it is to blame alcoholism or drug addiction on the victim is of course controversial. Not all initial addiction, we will simply assume, is itself blameless.

This line of argument unavoidably raises what we might loosely think of as a "statute of limitations" problem, or more precisely, a problem of what the law calls proximate causation. We may clarify the problem by reference to a different context, that of unemployment compensation. Let us suppose that the law generally provides unemployment compensation benefits to eligible workers, but denies those benefits to workers whose job loss is said to reflect their own fault. Now imagine a large employer that has just routinely and predictably laid off 10 percent of its workers, all those whose jobs require only the lowest level of skills. No court would deny unemployment compensation to any affected workers on the grounds, say, that they easily could have obtained job skills that would have protected them from being laid off, and that they knew or should have known this. Yet one might consider the layoff of at least some of these workers partly the workers' own fault. They might, given our assumptions, have easily avoided being laid off.

Not only relevant intervening events, but the mere passage of time seems to make a difference in evaluating these sorts of cases. Suppose a worker is chosen to be laid off because he frequently drinks on the job, and as a result makes poor-quality goods. Let us assume that a court would conclude that in such a case, the layoff is largely the fault of the worker, and would deny unemployment compensation.

But the court might reach this result only because of the close connection in time between the assumedly culpable behavior of drinking on the job and the resulting poor production. What if it could be shown clearly that the same poor quality production was due not to some contemporary behavior, but to equally culpable behavior by the worker that occurred, and ended, some years ago, which at the time could reasonably be foreseen to lead to poor future job performance? What if, for example, the worker knowingly took an illegal drug many years ago that could reasonably have been foreseen to cause temporary lapses in job performance years later?

In such a case, it is less clear that the courts would deny unemployment compensation on the view that the worker's unemployment was his own fault. After some lapse of time, culpable mistakes may count as less culpable, even if their causal relevance to one's present circumstances is clear. Of course, a court might seek to avoid this problem by attempting to find some more recent relevant personal fault. Perhaps there was available to the illegal drug taker some medical treatment that could have prevented or minimized future lapses in job performance. If so, the courts might fault the worker not merely for the initial reckless and illegal act, but for failing more recently to pursue treatment.

Similar issues arise with respect to the necessity defense. The courts, we may assume, would not recognize such a defense in the case of a person whose homelessness or subsequent illegal act was substantially their own fault. We may assume for purposes of argument that some homelessness and "theft of housing" reflect culpable initial acts of drinking or illegal drug taking, even if any later alcoholism or addiction is not in itself considered blameworthy. There may, however, be a reluctance to blame a homeless person for their mistakes if those mistakes were committed only some years ago. This reluctance to blame may be reinforced if the alcoholic or addicted homeless person has, in the meantime, sought and been denied treatment. Thus in such cases, no clear, bright rule can tell us precisely when a homeless person's prior behavior will disqualify her from pursuing a necessity defense.

Just as in the bread theft and illegal begging cases, however, a necessity defense will be denied to a homeless person who, the above complications aside, had reasonably available some practical alternative to acting illegally in order to protect life or health. This will normally be an interesting question of policy and fact. We would of course lose legal sympathy for Jean Valjean if it turned out that he could have liquidated some stock holdings, or if he had rejected a timely job offer out of caprice. Similar issues arise with respect to homelessness and the alternatives to homelessness.

The most obvious possible alternative to illegally avoiding homelessness is, of course, accommodation at a shelter run by a municipal government or a private charity. One possible judicial course is to simply hold, once and for all, that in the eyes of the law, some such legal alternative to homelessness is always available. Such a rule would, however, sacrifice realism. A legal alternative shelter facility may not in fact exist, or may not be reasonably knowable to the homeless defendant, or the facility may simply be full.

Even if such a shelter is available, we may not wish to judicially require its use via a criminal sanction. The very fact that some homeless persons prefer to sleep outside in cold weather rather than use a shelter should lead us to ask why. Often, the answer relates to the character of the shelter in question. The temperature inside the shelter may itself approach one extreme or another. Bedding materials may be unavailable. Where such materials are available, they may, to an imagination-staggering extent, be insect infested or copiously bloodied, in such a way as to call their conduciveness to health into question. Conditions in the bathroom may, to avoid further graphic depiction, be such as to provoke Dante to detailed note taking. The floor may be littered with used hypodermic needles, contrary, presumably, to appropriate hygienic standards. The danger of theft of one's few possessions, perhaps including prescription medicines, may be substantial. One's neighbors, inches from one's bed, may be hostile or deranged. All in all, a mental image of a homeless shelter as essentially a civilian version of an army barracks or akin to a crowded nursing home is thus not invariably accurate.[13]

How should the law respond if a sufficient shelter is available but is unknown to the arrested homeless person, or if the homeless person refuses to avail herself of a legal alternative, on grounds the law deems inadequate? These issues raise the problem of subjective versus objective standards of knowledge and reasonableness, with regard to persons whose capacities and judgments may often be at some remove from our own.

This problem is complicated by our inability to imagine what it must genuinely be like to be chronically, desperately poor or homeless if our personal experience with such conditions is limited. Even the great novelists must in this again fail, if only because of the inherent limitations of their medium. This inevitable failure may have legally and humanly unfortunate implications. Reading a great literary description of an impoverished or desperate life may tempt us to imagine, preposterously, that we now fully appreciate the stunting, deformative, pervasive effects that early and chronic poverty or desperation may have on a life. We again fill in gaps and uncertainties with our own projected experiences. As a result, we underappreciate the magnitude of those effects. Our misperception then naturally leads to an insufficiently sympathetic response, as we take the lives of the poor and desperate to more closely resemble our own experience than is genuinely accurate.

More specifically, given our inability to fully empathize with the desperate, we will naturally tend to assume that choices are obvious and practical for the homeless when they may in fact not be. As much as it may be in the immediate, vital interest of the homeless to know of practical, legally available shelter possibilities, for example, the homeless may not see their environment with the advantages of middle-class resources, backgrounds, and perspectives.

Reasonable minds may differ, in general or in particular cases, as to what it is appropriate to expect homeless persons to know and believe, beyond what they actually, subjectively happen to know and believe. We need not argue that the law must take the homeless as they are in all their subjective detail, or even that the law must, by way of compromise, fashion a "reasonable homeless person" standard for the knowledge, judgments, and capacities the law will expect of the homeless.

There may in rare cases be, for example, mentally ill but legally competent homeless persons who are genuinely unaware of a particular reasonable and legal alternative to sleeping in a public park. There may, in such cases, thus be no genuine necessity objectively underlying their illegal sleeping in the park. The law may wish to assume that such persons really should have known of such legal alternatives, or that their ignorance of such alternatives, even if reasonable, is irrelevant. But this poses a difficult issue.

At a minimum, the law should not deny that some significant differences may exist, on matters of knowledge, resources, and capacities, between some homeless persons and the rest of us. Refusing to acknowledge any such differences winds up imposing middle-class standards inappropriately. The homeless have every incentive to learn of alternatives to sleeping in the park. But they may not have been told of or have otherwise learned of such alternatives. Homelessness is simply not, in this sense, a class-neutral phenomenon. Not being middle-class is inseparable from homelessness. Judging the homeless entirely by distinctively middle-class standards is, in a word, a travesty.

It is one thing to impose reasonable and realistic demands on persons. A reasonable challenge may lead to unexpectedly positive results. But it does no honor either to the law or to the homeless to assume, to the criminal detriment of homeless defendants, that they are capable of what is beyond any reasonable expectation of attainment. Demanding more of the homeless than they are reasonably capable of delivering adds not to their dignity, but to their degradation. As a society, we are ready enough to fault parents or employers who, pathologically, demand what their children or employees cannot reasonably deliver. We recognize such behavior as ultimately reflecting underlying conflicts within the person imposing such demands.

The legal system should not, on a larger scale, be permitted the same self-serving error. If the legal system or the government prefers that its citizenry universally meet certain minimum standards of civic competence, it should promote, or remove privately and publicly created obstacles to, such universal competence. The legal system should not simply pretend that such a desirable state of affairs already obtains.

This is as much an issue of fairness as of logic. Just as a city with a limited or shrinking tax base might resent the unfairness of having to bear the costs of public homeless shelters without the assistance of the state, neighboring states, or the federal government, so a homeless person might resent the unfairness of being suddenly promoted, for criminal law purposes only, to the status of a deemed exhibitor of middle-class capacities.

Certainly, if homeless persons who illegally obtain alternative housing could, in some cases, themselves be said to be acting unfairly with regard to other homeless or distressed persons, that unfairness would be legally relevant to accepting or rejecting a necessity defense. In some cases, claims that a homeless person's illegal act was unfair to other desperate persons, even if no more intrusive or any broader than necessary, might not be entirely fanciful.

But this should not be presumed to be particularly common. It might, admittedly, be claimed that a homeless person who has taken the initiative, for example, by "squatting" in abandoned or run-down public housing units has jumped the queue and deprived perhaps equally deserving persons of public housing. Others may have patiently waited on line for scarce public housing for years.

If the squatter's case is really one of desperation and homelessness, rising to the level of a genuine emergency threatening life or health, we must ask whether those patiently waiting for scarce public housing can assert the same degree of desperation. If so, we may then ask whether the squatter's illegal act really sets up some direct conflict of interest with those equally desperate persons. The space within a room is, after all, typically shareable. More than one genuinely desperate and necessitous person can be accommodated within squatters' housing, and the illegal act of squatting may even productively call political attention to the insufficiency of public housing, thereby benefiting others.

Of course, a duty of fairness is also owed by illegal housing occupants to the rest of society, including the amply housed, as well. Fairness, as an element of a legitimate necessity defense, requires that the defendant not have burdened unduly or unnecessarily the moral rights, legitimate expectations, and privacy interests of residential and commercial property owners. Thus there will typically be no necessity for squatters to occupy spare bedrooms of residential homeowners or office space in ongoing commercial enterprises. No necessity for this exists because less intrusive and disruptive alternatives exist. We are of course assuming the legitimacy of the current distribution of property rights.

This restriction on the necessity defense parallels those regarding other conduct we have examined. If one is starving, a loaf of bread is no less suited to one's life or health interests than would be a more burdensome, intrusive, disruptive, or "broader" theft of exotic pheasant eggs. If one must beg, it may not be necessary to beg inside the elevators of public buildings, for similar reasons. Similarly, it should commonly be possible for homeless persons to protect their life or health interests through some sort of shelter without becoming the roommates of unconsenting leaseholders.

This is not to suggest, however, that allowing a necessity defense for the homeless would reduce overall freedom. We may stipulate that allowing the homeless to seek refuge even in an unused warehouse or other commercial facility reduces the freedom of the property owner. But in an at least equally valid, basic, and familiar sense of the word "freedom," our necessitous homeless are themselves unfree insofar as they are exposed to arrest or conviction if they seek shelter. In the meantime, the range of reasonably valued actions and choices legally open to the involuntarily homeless is quite constrictively narrow. Thus the narrow freedom, in a traditional sense, of the involuntarily homeless.

How, then, does the law currently react to those who, without relevant fault, find themselves homeless and who then, out of necessity, engage in some illegal survival- or health-preservative conduct? We will assume that the defendant has actually chosen voluntarily to engage in the illegal conduct. But it should be remembered that there is as well an even more brute form of necessity. A homeless person may wind up illegally sleeping in a public park not as a result of choice, but out of sheer exhaustion. In the extreme, the body simply permits no further movement or reflection on options, and involuntarily shuts down, even under circumstances violative of the law.

Generally, the law is not accommodating of even the most innocent, conscientious, and desperately necessitous squatter. A squatter has no legally recognized property interest. Squatters generally cannot bootstrap themselves into possessing such an interest, even for purposes of due process or search and seizure privacy rights, by an illegal entry. Nor, generally, is this result changed if the defendants make voluntary repairs or improvements to the property.

The Constitution, as authoritatively interpreted, does not recognize any rights that would change these results. The Supreme Court has recognized no constitutional right to housing. The Court's basic conclusion has been that "we do not denigrate the importance of decent, safe, and sanitary housing. But the Constitution does not provide judicial remedies for every social and economic ill. We are unable to perceive in that document any constitutional guarantee of access to dwellings of a particular quality."[14]

Of course, many homeless defendants are arrested for seeking housing that falls short of the decent, safe, and sanitary. Such cases are far from any judicial involvement in arbitrary, subjective disputes over whether particular living conditions count as genuinely decent, safe, and sanitary. The Court's real concern, however, seems to be with the reach or scope of the Constitution. From the idea that the Constitution cannot fix everything that is broken in society, the Court wishes to conclude that no constitutional right is at stake in dying of exposure to the cold a few yards away from a technically closed public shelter. Thus while we are presumed, as drafters and ratifiers of the Constitution, to have cared strongly about the quartering of troops in our home, we are also presumed to have been legally indifferent to the risk of having no home of any sort at all. The Constitution's message to the involuntarily homeless is thus that while needlessly dying of exposure is not of constitutional significance, the interests jeopardized by the presence of troops in one's real or nonexistent home are.

The class bias, or class-differential impact, of such a constitutional analysis is not difficult to detect. But there is sometimes a certain gingerliness in recognizing that denying rights to, or imposing legal burdens on, the homeless is not a class-neutral policy. In one of the most interesting recent homelessness cases, the restrictive ordinance at stake was referred to as an "anti-camping" ordinance, intended to prohibit "camping" and the storing of one's personal property in public places.[15] The problem perceived by the city in this case was actually not, as we might imagine, hordes of unruly Cub Scouts tenting overnight in public parks, indifferent to the protests of city officials, or any other aspect of the largely middle-class phenomenon of camping. There are the desperate and involuntary homeless, and there are campers. The two groups, to put the matter as mildly as possible, do not coincide.

Judicial concern for homeless squatters is, of course, not difficult to find. The problem, however, is that such concern often takes ironic, if not perverse, forms. In one case, a group of homeless persons occupied abandoned city property and, according to their own testimony, made a number of important long-term improvements to the building, including the installation of pipes, wiring, and a circuit breaker box.[16] In evicting the formerly homeless, the court was able, in effect, to hold these repairs and improvements against them, out of a concern for their well-being. This judicial maneuver was accomplished by noting the absence of any proof that the repairs and improvements were done safely. For all that had been established in the case, the installed wiring, or with some irony, the circuit breaker box itself, might lead to an electrical fire, jeopardizing the welfare of the squatters.

It should be remembered that the building was formerly unoccupied and abandoned, so that the risk to cotenants of any fire was non-existent. While there may have been tenants in adjoining build-ings, we must not start from the assumption that the baseline risk of fire in an utterly abandoned building is zero. Thus what is most strik-ing is the court's willingness, in the absence of any evidence regard-ing the safety or unsafety of the repairs, to second-guess and overrule the occupants on matters largely of their own physical safety.

As we have seen, many homeless persons exhibit only imperfect rationality. But a group of homeless persons may reasonably be cred-ited with grasping the risk of fire. Perhaps the repairs were compe-tently done. Perhaps they were not. But the occupants of the premis-es were at least as interested in their own safety as an appellate court. It is entirely possible that the tenants could have decided that the risk of injury from a fire was insufficient to tip the balance in favor of their next best housing alternative, which may have been either the same facility without wiring, or the street.

Thus not all the elements of a reasonable judgment as to safety may have been before the court. Setting aside the issue of fires, there are also considerations such as temperature and wind exposure, assaults, rodent and insect bites, and so forth. In these matters, the chronically homeless may have direct experience. And in the absence of a complete record, it is not necessary for courts to guess in which direction genuine compassion lies, especially over the apparent dis-sent of those persons most directly affected.

If the conditions under which the homeless would otherwise have to live are sufficiently nightmarish, the option of jail or imprison-ment may not, at the very least, seem much worse. Some jail condi-tions may indeed beat the public park. But jail should never be judi-cially presented as a counterproposal to a desperate defendant who does not seek out jail, as those pleading necessity presumably would not. Jail is intentionally stigmatizing and officially condemnatory. This cannot be balanced off against the availability of meals in prison. The claim of the absence of reasonable alternative housing should not be held to include incarceration, thereby trapping the homeless defendant between going to jail as an alternative to homelessness, and going to jail as a sentence following the rejection of one's necessity defense.

Courts should thus not hold out the unchosen option of having gone to jail as the reason for subsequently jailing the defendant. There is, after all, a judicial and moral difference between even an abandoned building and a jail. Nor is the difference merely a matter of the concrete experiences associated with the two. Occupants of abandoned buildings are, admittedly, in some fashion themselves stigmatized. But a jail term is, and is officially intended to be, a morally stigmatizing and deliberately punitive official response to criminal acts. Prison is, generally, for culpable transgressors. No state has the moral standing to say that rather than sleep even illegally in the park, or in an abandoned building, thereby risking arrest and trial, one should have committed some other illegal act with the intention of being arrested and jailed for the sake of jail housing.

Interestingly, the state often does not respond to trespasses by the homeless in a judicially straightforward way. Often, the homeless are not tried, allowed to present any arguably appropriate defense, and then acquitted or convicted and sentenced. Instead, the process is short-circuited. Homeless persons are, apparently, often arrested and then released before any trial occurs.[17] Whether this process reflects official benevolence need not be addressed. The arrest itself may involve real costs to the homeless if, as is apparently common, it leads to the loss of their scant personal property, or if it impairs their ability to make appealing legal sleeping arrangements for the evening. And, in the absence of a trial, the arrestee loses the most direct and obvious opportunity to raise and perhaps establish a necessity defense for at least some homelessness cases, where a recognized necessity defense might limit the practice of arresting and releasing the homeless.

Where the necessity defense in homelessness cases is allowed to be argued, the result and judicial logic tend to parallel that of the court in the *Moe* food theft case. The typical judicial reaction is one of discomfort and concern for the overextension of any such defense. The potential for abuse is declared to be severe. One court for example, has recently argued that "if one's homeless status entitled one to evade prosecution for removing waste from trash receptacles in order to find something to eat or wear, it is not difficult to rationalize constitutional protection for stealing food or clothing."[18]

Probably the leading case in this area of the law is *Southwark London Borough Council v. Williams*, an English appellate case from 1971.[19] There were several defendants in these combined cases, and as it turns out, only the Williamses were actually homeless before the charged offense. The defendants had made an illegal but orderly entry into empty housing stock owned by the Borough Council of Southwark. The defendants' entry into and occupancy of the premises could be said to have jumped a queue of almost 9,000 persons on the local public housing waiting list. On the other hand, the housing in question had been officially classified, evidently, as not reasonably repairable or fit for occupancy for at least some time into the future. The premises had in any event been boarded up for some time. The defendants had, apparently, made significant repairs to the property promoting health during the course of their occupancy.

The court, through Lord Denning, then took up the possibility of a necessity defense in such cases. Lord Denning recognized some case law allowing an encroachment on private property rights in case of great and imminent danger to life under emergency circumstances. But such a legal defense must, in Lord Denning's judgment, be kept carefully and narrowly limited. Caution must be exercised, lest the door be flung open, disastrously, to many excuses in many cases. Thus the conviction of three shipwrecked sailors accused of murder and cannibalism of a cabin boy even to save their own lives under necessitous circumstances.[20]

Lord Denning then rejected a necessity defense for a starving man who enters a house in order to take food for the purpose of self-preservation. But the possible distinction between a house and a retail store, or even a vending machine, was evidently not of much consequence. The scope of Lord Denning's reasoning accommodates all such circumstances, and homelessness as well as starvation. Admitting a necessity defense in such cases "would open a way through which all kinds of disorder and lawlessness would pass. . . . If homelessness were once admitted as a defense to trespass, no one's house would be safe. . . . There would be others who would imagine that they were in need, or would invent a need, so as to gain entry . . . . So the courts must, for the sake of law and order, take a firm stand. They must refuse to admit the plea of necessity to the hungry and the homeless: and trust that their distress will be relieved by the charitable and the good."[21]

To this, Edmund Davies, L.J., added that the unfortunate circumstance in which the defendants had found themselves was not really an emergency, but a long-standing, if difficult, state of affairs. Megaw, L.J., also concurred, observing that the defendants' actions could be said to be undemocratic, in that they amounted to an unauthorized overturning of the democratically arrived at terms of the local public housing policy.

There is much that may be said in reply to the court's logic in this case. The most important responses are by now obvious. The court rests most of its argument on the fear of eventual abuse and overextension of a necessity defense in these sorts of cases. For the most part, the court's argument is not that a necessity defense could never be appropriate in a case taken in isolation. Thus the court's reasoning must largely be judged by the reasonableness of its fears for future cases. How likely is significant abuse, overextension, and consequent disorder if a necessity defense were recognized in otherwise appropriate cases? In particular, could the courts craft usable rules providing for a necessity defense in such cases, but discouraging or excluding such a defense, and the underlying criminal conduct, in improper cases?

It is difficult to avoid this kind of question. Any defense, including that of self-defense and insanity, is subject to some degree of abuse and overextension. Tort claims against close family members, where the real financial compensation is from insurance policy proceeds, are also subject to abuse and overextension. Recovery for mental suffering in general, or for the negligent infliction of emotional distress, may also invite abuse and overextension. But we still assume that it is on balance worth recognizing these kinds of defenses and claims.

The question then is one of the likely degree and controllability, at reasonable cost, of overextension and abuse of the defense, particularly in cases of severe abuse. The costs of borderline abuses, after all, may not be high, even if those cases are relatively frequent. This is of course a large empirical and policy-driven inquiry. But a few obvious points may be made.

First, in a society of the wealth and charity relied on by Lord Denning, most persons will simply not be near a socioeconomic position in which a starvation or homelessness-based necessity defense can be invoked with any plausibility. For most of us, the costs and rewards of stealing a loaf of bread, or of breaking into abandoned, unwired housing, bearing in mind the risk of a jury's not accepting a necessity defense under our circumstances, seem rather unattractive.

Much of the jury's inquiry, after all, consists not in speculatively probing states of mind, but in examining fairly objective and reasonably cheaply determinable circumstances. Most of us, after all, have a box of crackers on the shelf, a checking account, or an available relative willing to share food. The existence or nonexistence of legal alternatives to necessitous crimes is mainly an objective matter, and even their reasonable availability is largely objective. Thus a merely imagined need can normally be exposed as such.

An invented need is, of course, merely invented, and not a genuine case of necessity. If a defendant intentionally, or even carelessly, places herself in a position where only illegal acts will save her life or health, her intent or carelessness should be no less provable to the jury than in any typical intentional or negligent tort case. Even for most persons who are already not particularly well off, the incentives for placing oneself in the position of being able to make a plausible claim of necessity, with respect to food or shelter, are minimal indeed.

Lord Denning's alarm over the prospect of hungry burglars raiding one's home refrigerator or slumbering in one's guest room may safely be minimized or dismissed entirely. A necessity defense may be written on such terms as we like. The defendant may, for example, be required to bear the burden of proof on all issues relevant to the necessity defense. While it is impossible for a defendant to strictly prove a negative, as that no alternative was available, the defendant may typically be better placed to meaningfully discuss the presence or absence of alternatives, and their reasonableness, than the government.

If we care to, we may also judicially establish a fixed, reasonable presumption that the hungry or exhausted had available to them some alternative to residential trespass, or that it is their fault if they did not. The same limitation could also be imposed legislatively, by statute. Thus if we wish, we may make Lord Denning's fears virtually groundless. The legal incentive to unconsentedly enter a private residence raised by the necessity defense would then be essentially zero. In the odd case, a defendant might attempt to argue that she mistakenly assumed the building to not be a residence, and that this mistake should be excused or ignored, but this hardly opens the door to the sort of assault on privacy and residential property rights feared by Lord Denning.

Justice Davies's view of the defendants' plight as chronic, as opposed to an emergency, also deserves some response. Strictly, we may say, it is mistaken or irrelevant. An emergency that persists, without losing its severity or its necessity, does not cease to be an emergency as it becomes chronic. We may think of it as a chronic emergency. Of course, there is real substance to Davies's point. Duration can be relevant to necessity, but duration need not destroy necessity. As a rule of thumb, we may suppose that the longer an emergency persists, the less reasonable it is to fail to find some legal alternative to coping illegally with that emergency. While finding some food to eat is, for some of us, a new problem each day, we may reasonably be asked to draw upon the knowledge and experience we have gained in previous searches for food.

Thus at best, the chronic nature of an emergency may cast doubt on the defendant's claim that no reasonable and available alternative existed to the defendant's illegal response to that emergency. But genuine necessity does not always dissolve over any given time frame. The necessity may even tighten its grip. A homeless person may, over time, find more shelters closing than opening, or fewer incidental job opportunities available rather than more. Homelessness itself tends to diminish one's opportunities. Hunger or malnutrition, along with exposure to the elements, may naturally worsen in their effects with the passage of time.

It must be admitted, in response to the observations of Justice Megaw, that there is indeed something undemocratic about violating a democratically established housing policy. We may simply assume that all homeless adults have a genuine and fair opportunity to vote and otherwise influence the democratic process of policy formation. Certainly a public housing policy is unlikely to provide for illegal occupancy. But we can hardly infer from the absence of such a provision that the council, or the citizenry generally, would reject a necessity defense under the most extreme set of facts. What if a middle-class business person were faultlessly driven, by a looming tornado, to briefly seek shelter in abandoned public housing stock? Can we infer democratic disapproval of such a necessitous act? Any necessity defense at all, even for hikers blamelessly stranded by violent storms, may involve something of an exception to a democratically endorsed system of property rights. At trial, a jury might express popular, democratic community sentiment as well in endorsing a necessity defense. And in an appropriate case, as where the housing in question is not actively slated for repair and restoration to the available public housing stock, the effect of illegal squatting on the interests of those waiting for public housing may be minimal, or even favorable.

Of course, a housing authority may have had sound reasons for boarding up the facility in question. The structure may be dangerous. But it is again doubtful how much the law should second-guess the judgments of necessitous squatters, at least with respect to obvious dangers, on matters of the squatters' own health and safety. Even a boarded-up facility, with or without the squatters' repairs and labor investments, may beat the squatters' next best legal or illegal option. If we wish, the law can protect the public interest, and perhaps discourage unnecessary risk taking, by providing that necessitous squatters, in entering upon boarded-up property, waive all claims for injuries, short- or long-term, against any party. The risks of necessitous squatting would, if the courts opted for this rule, thus not be shiftable to unconsenting, unsuspecting parties.

Finally, let us briefly address Lord Denning's concluding remark that the courts must, instead of admitting a necessity defense, trust that the desperation of those in the defendants' position will be relieved by charity. It is quite possible that this remark is not intended to add anything of substance to the legal analysis already presented by Denning. Perhaps he is simply acknowledging that just this sort of trust is what is left for the judiciary and for the desperate after the doors to a necessity defense have been closed.

If, on the other hand, Lord Denning seeks to imply that the practical need for a necessity defense is minimal, due to the expansive and effective efforts of governmental and charitable organizations, he is writing against the evidence. As the *Williams* case itself suggests, it is possible to fall through the British governmental and charitable safety net, to a position of desperation. And the problem of unaddressed vital needs among the homeless has, at least in the United States, only grown since the publication of Lord Denning's opinion in *Williams*.

But can anything else be said to ease Lord Denning's concerns? We can point out that the practical incentive to abuse different sorts of legal opportunities is far from uniform. One who takes advantage of an indulgent legal rule to defraud an insurance carrier of a large sum of money may well have a strong incentive to do so. But a carefully crafted necessity defense, extending admittedly beyond the scope with which Lord Denning is judicially comfortable, sets up no comparable incentive. Any middle- or working-class person who stole bread or minimal housing, absent real necessity and out of a selfish desire to personally profit, relying on the possibility of abusing a necessity defense to avoid the costs and stigma of criminal conviction, might well be better off exploring a defense of insanity.

The potential for creativity in the criminal law should not be overlooked. Courts might, for example, consider that one who is in a position of blameless necessity may not remain in such desperate straits. A job opportunity may arise, or a disability, social security, or welfare check may begin to provide a steady stream of income. There is no reason a necessity defense could not be qualified by taking into account the defendant's income at the time of trial. The defendant would be legally required to make restitution if financially able to do so for any direct pecuniary costs, such as the price of a stolen loaf of bread, incurred by private parties as a result of the defendant's necessitous acts. The defendant's ability to pay such costs, in whole or in part, would be judged, of course, at the time of trial, and not at the time of the necessitous offense.

Admittedly, this would mean that a criminal defendant could know the law, but not her precise eventual liability or obligations under the law, at the time of the offense. But it is hardly clear why this sort of legal arrangement must violate the defendant's due process or fair trial rights. After all, criminal defendants accused of theft may be liable civilly for torts of conversion or trespass as well. And in general, punishments are knowable only within broad ranges at the time of the offense. There may, for some, nonetheless be a certain appeal to building limited restitutionary obligations into the fabric of the criminal law.

In the final part of our survey of the necessity defense to survival-oriented thefts, let us abstract from particular kinds of cases to consider the necessity defense, and its legal elements, by itself. Our technique will be eclectic. We will simply report findings from numerous legal sources that offer guidance on the necessity defense in general.

Let us consider, then, the legal defense of necessity in the abstract. We will thus consider what are called the elements of a necessity defense. The elements of a necessity defense are the separate components—states of affairs, circumstances, or states of mind—that must be jointly shown to establish a valid defense of necessity. The courts, with or without the assistance of the commentators, actually do not agree unanimously on what must be shown for a necessity defense to be valid. But there is certainly enough common ground among the cases for a coherent discussion, and if the most demanding, restrictive cases are included, the discussion itself will also be fair.

Most of the basic elements of a necessity defense will be easily recognized from our discussion of the necessity defense in several specific contexts above. Courts often begin the list of elements by referring to what we may call an "imminence" requirement. This element requires something like the "clear and present danger" that must famously be shown if speech critical of a government may properly be restricted. Generally, in the context of necessity, a specific threat of an immediate harm must be shown. The harm must not be a merely speculative possibility, a merely future or long-term risk, or fairly debatable as to its very existence in the first place.

The imminence requirement certainly seems sensible. The starving or health-jeopardized homeless persons on which we have focused should, in appropriate cases, be capable of meeting such a requirement. But in a way, "imminence" in a literal sense is only a proxy for what we are ideally interested in. Ideally, our concern is not so much with imminence as with the unavoidability of the injury.

Suppose, however unrealistically, that we could know today that a person will inevitably die of scurvy in exactly two weeks, and no sooner, unless a lemon is stolen today, and no later. Thus we assume that today is actually the last chance to avert a death two weeks hence. Such a death is not literally imminent. But if we are willing to accept a necessity defense in cases of imminent harm, it is difficult to reject a necessity defense in a case of nonimminent but otherwise inevitable harm.

We live, however, in a world in which the second best is often a better guide than the ideal. So it may be that an imminence requirement is actually valuable, perhaps in reducing the potential for abuse and misjudgment. If we require that the harm be imminent, we avoid the possible mistake of believing, erroneously, that some future harm will inevitably occur unless some illegal act is undertaken. Some surprising turn of events may occur, in which starvation is warded off. This might occur through charity, a job offer, an unrelated criminal conviction, or eligibility for a welfare program. And the more imminent the harm, the clearer will be the genuineness, severity, and inevitability of the harm in the absence of an illegal act.

The courts and commentators then typically go on to require that the necessitousness of the defendant's circumstances not have been brought about by the defendant. This requirement refers not only to the defendant's underlying need but to the absence of any reasonable legal alternative, as where charity will not suffice, but theft will. The defense is thus unavailable if the defendant has blameworthily put herself in the position of starving, or blameworthily reduced her means of avoiding starvation to illegal options only.

This is, as we have seen above, a difficult issue on which we have little to add at a more abstract, general level. Standard tort law teaches us that fault can be shared, that more than one person may be fully responsible for some state of affairs, and that fault comes in degrees, ranging from slight carelessness or lack of reasonableness through recklessness and premeditation. We should, however, point out that not all thefts intended to avoid starvation are committed by the person who anticipates starving. In fact, the more imminent the death or disability from starvation, the less likely the victim is to be capable of theft. It is thus not merely a matter of romantic sentimentality or propaganda value that both Valjean and Nanet steal loaves of bread for the sake of other persons.

What, then, if the persons on whose behalf Valjean and Nanet steal bread were clearly responsible for their own dire need, as through sheer laziness? Shouldn't this responsibility carry over to Valjean and Nanet? If not, couldn't those we may consider to be undeserving starvers immunize themselves by inducing some innocent third party to steal on their behalf? We thus have some reason to believe that the fault of the starver should be imputed to third party rescuers.

But the matter is not quite so simple. Some third party rescuers, perhaps even close relatives of the starvers, may not know, and may have no reason to know, of the starving person's culpability. In such a case, it might be morally more attractive to convict the undeserving starver of conspiracy to steal, if the starver knows of and approves of the theft in advance, and to acquit the actual thief on grounds of necessity, even though the starver had no valid necessity defense to transfer. Do we really wish to convict someone who, given no alternative, steals water for a dangerously dehydrated stranger, where the rescuer has no reason to know that, say, the dehydrated stranger has recently escaped from and could have quite safely returned to prison?

We need not take a position on this issue. Murkiness may be unavoidable here, as the person who is starving or otherwise necessitous may not know the law relating to necessity, and may not know that the law would judge her responsible for her own desperate straits. Or what if the starver does not approve in advance the theft on her behalf, but is said to "ratify" or approve of the theft after the fact? If a starving person is presented with bread, does the desperate act of merely eating what she knows to be stolen bread ratify the theft, exposing her to some sort of criminal liability?

Some aspects of the problem, however, seem clear enough. For example, the actual thief should not be allowed to hide behind the ignorance of an innocent, starving person. Let us assume that the starving person does not know of, and has no way of knowing of, any legal channel for obtaining the bread. Clearly, this faultless ignorance should not automatically transfer to her rescuer. If her rescuer, for example, knows of a viable legal source for the bread, as through a nearby soup kitchen with a "no questions asked" take-out policy, the rescuer cannot be immunized by the starver's own faultless ignorance of this option if the rescuer chooses to steal the bread instead.

The possibility of "standing" rescue groups poses additional problems. If a broad rule is necessary, it may be best to rule out a necessity defense where the illegal act is done by even a well-intentioned preexisting group organized for such purposes. While such groups would introduce certain efficiencies, they would also tend to lack knowledge of the real personal circumstances of the arguably necessitous victim, and might ultimately amount to an illegal equivalent of just one more charity or social service agency, with practical accessibility problems of their own.

The discussion of these issues of blameworthiness itself raises a further general element of the necessity defense. This element requires something like the absence of legal alternative means of avoiding the harm to the defendant. Additionally, the law requires something like the absence of other illegal, but less offensive, less burdensome, or less intrusive ways of avoiding the harm as well.

Thus, as we have seen above, a necessity defense will probably not be available for breaking into an occupied residence in search of bread if the defendant knew of an unattended vending machine that would accept a slug or a washer in the defendant's possession. At its strictest, the law may want to require that the defendant have committed only the least serious otherwise criminal act.

Of course, the least serious otherwise illegal act that would avoid starvation in a given case may not be obvious. Sometimes, reasonably conscientious persons will disagree as to whether one possible crime is more serious than another. Which, for example, is worse: to moderately damage an unattended vending machine or to steal a loaf of bread as the unarmed store owner watches? Nor will all the viable legal and illegal alternatives always be evident to even the most knowledgeable person, let alone to a desperate, distraught, perhaps mentally ill defendant. Surely we should not require near-perfect knowledge on the part of a defendant whose very circumstances are linked to having or perceiving few options.

Thus the state should not be able to defeat a necessity defense merely by proving, for example, that an otherwise anonymous and undistinctive person would, if consulted, have legally supplied all the defendant's needs with promptness and courtesy. The law is willing enough to excuse a driver who violates the speed limit in order to transport a seriously injured person to a hospital. Presumably the law does not refuse the defense of necessity in such case if, unknown to the rescuer, another medical facility is available nearby, such that violating the speed limit is not strictly necessary. The poor and the desperate should be held to no higher standard in this respect.

What if a starving person falsely believes that a legal, or less seriously illegal, alternative exists, but chooses what is in fact the least seriously illegal course only out of malice or some other unjustifiable motive? Here again, a concern for the legitimate interests of the desperate need not dictate either result. A court might uphold the necessity defense claim on the grounds that, after all, the defendant chose what was in fact the least harmful course. On the other hand, if the defendant intended to inflict unnecessary suffering on other people, and if that intent cannot itself be somehow excused, a court might be more impressed by the defendant's malice than by the defendant's sheer luck in not causing any unnecessary harm, despite the defendant's intent to do so. In a literal sense, the desperate can live with either judicial result.

In some respects, the law of necessity presents complications that do not typically concern the desperate. Sometimes, for example, the courts adjudicate, and generally reject, a necessity defense in what might be called symbolic political protest cases. In such a case, typically, an organized political group may trespass on government or private property in an attempt to change some government policy or decision. Thus a group might trespass on a nuclear power plant facility or attempt to block the transportation of chemical or biological weapons.

In such cases, a necessity defense faces a number of judicial obstacles. But here we will concern ourselves with only two. First, it may hardly be clear that the otherwise illegal act undertaken by the protestors would, by itself, actually prevent the alleged harm from occurring, even for the immediate future. Government policies change slowly, if at all. And second, courts may point to the legally available political avenues for promoting social change, including legal demonstrations, lobbying, and voting. If a government policy changes, it may well be because of utterly legal dissent.

Whether the courts are right in analyzing the political protest cases along such lines is not of direct concern. Instead, we need merely recognize that these issues should typically loom less large in cases involving the genuinely desperate. No doubt we may read symbolic protest into a desperate act of begging, and the beggar may in a given case consciously entertain such thoughts. But desperation, by definition, is not exclusively symbolic. The desperate, for example, want concretely not to die, at least just now. If one steals and eats bread under desperate circumstances, one achieves, actually and not merely symbolically, at least one's short-term goal of staving off disaster.

Nor can courts always claim, with any plausibility, that a starving person should, instead of stealing a loaf of bread, have obtained food by means of legal political activity. This is a somewhat subtle point. Many courts consign the starving or homeless to whatever might result from legal political or nonpolitical activities. Typically enough, courts point to at least the abstract possibility of some sort of legal solution. This was, for example, the response of Lord Denning to the *Williams* defendants. But it would be simply implausible for the courts to make the further claim that had the defendant sought a legal solution, she would have actually found legally available food or shelter on the occasion in question. That Marie Antoinette holds up the possibility of eating cake does not mean that cake is actually available. We cannot stop a court from pointing, if it wishes, to legal public housing that is already spoken for, and not realistically available to the defendant. But a court's pointing to the existence of public housing does not mean that a unit is actually vacant and available for the defendant.

Let us turn, then, to a further general element of the necessity defense. We have at least implicitly addressed this element above, but it deserves some attention in a broader setting. Typically, the courts require a balancing of affected interests, or an inquiry into proportionality. Roughly, the idea is that the harm avoided by the defendant's otherwise illegal act must be proportionate to, or must clearly outweigh, the harms flowing from that otherwise illegal act. The defendant's otherwise illegal act must, in a word, have been "worth it."

This apparently simple idea masks, unfortunately, a number of complications. Let us begin by noting that this element appears to invite us to weigh the harms of an otherwise illegal act against the harms associated with potentially quite legal acts, such as dying of malnutrition or exposure. Thus some legal harm may somehow outweigh some illegal harm. Actually, a few courts have required that the harm sought to be avoided by the otherwise illegal act be itself illegal. Thus one might be permitted to commit a battery to prevent a murder. This interpretation would restrict the necessity defense to cases of otherwise illegal acts committed to prevent proportionately serious crimes.

If the necessity defense is to be restricted in such a fashion, it would come perilously close to a redundant overlap with established, uncontroversial defenses such as self-defense, defense of others, and defense of property. There is certainly a sense in which we might call warding off starvation or exposure an act of self-defense. But we cannot bring our desperate necessity cases under the notion of defense of life or health without substantially expanding the standard legal idea of self-defense. In a society dominated by impersonal markets and large bureaucracies, most people who develop serious malnutrition or who suffer from exposure are not being threatened, intentionally or otherwise, by an individual actor or discrete group of actors. This is unlike the established self-defense cases. More typical-ly, the homeless are simply unknown to the powerful, or are the objects of indifference. We shall have a bit more to say about per-sonal, impersonal, and "natural" threats a bit further below.

In the meantime, we need only note that if the necessity defense encompassed only illegal threats, some of the most obvious and uncontroversially valid necessity defense cases would be clearly ruled out. It is, for example, not illegal for a storm to trap a hiker in life-threatening circumstances. It is not illegal for a storm at sea to "threaten" to sink a ship unless some cargo is necessitously jetti-soned. It is not illegal for an acute viral infection to "attack" a person, necessitating a violation of the speed limit in transporting that per-son to a doctor. But if we deny a necessity defense in all such cases, we have dramatically curtailed the traditional scope of the necessity defense without satisfactory explanation.

At an abstract level, the requirement of weighing harms or inter-ests and making determinations of proportionality can be daunting. Let us consider merely a few examples. First, we may simply not be sure what we are doing when we try to weigh the harm of death or jeopardized health against the "harm," moral and social, of a crime. This we may call the problem of commensurability. How much, if any, "weight" should be attached to the violation of the law in itself, apart from any bad consequences of violating the law?

If we do focus on consequences, we may be unsure whether to consider more than any given individual case. In an isolated case, preservation of the defendant's health may seem to clearly outweigh the minimal damage done to property rights or the system of laws by the defendant's crime. But it might be less clear that frequent preser-vation of many defendants' health by frequent commission of crimes involves the same proportionality. If crime becomes too frequent, a "tipping point" may be reached at which the harm to the system of laws suddenly becomes dramatically worse.

We must also ask how intellectually ambitious the weighing process is supposed, in practice, to be. Are we to strive as fully as possible toward an ideal of considering all harms and benefits, direct and indirect, short- and long-term, to all potentially affected persons? Would we, on the other hand, actually be better off refusing to speculate as to some harms and benefits? What are we to do with the fact that many harms and benefits are not absolutely certain to occur? Should we discount, or reduce the weight of, outcomes that are likely but not certain?

After all, a hiker who breaks into a building to escape a blizzard may, given the circumstances, be exchanging certain imminent death for certain short-term survival and a long life expectancy. On the other hand, many of our starvers and homeless may face reduced life expectancies whether they are, for example, able to break into abandoned housing or not. Someone who barely avoids starvation today may tend to be the sort of person who may also face starvation again next week. Living in the public park may be hazardous to one's health. But living in abandoned housing, even if a significant improvement over the park, hardly guarantees against serious housing-related health problems. The act of breaking into an unheated building may thus significantly improve one's chances, while not ensuring health or survival.

We may wish to factor in the possibility that the defendant's illegal act may turn out to have been in vain, or to have "bought" only a limited additional period of health. But to reject a necessity defense in such a case, on the grounds that the illegal act did not reasonably guarantee the defendant's health or survival, seems rather insensitive. One would, in effect, be holding the extreme desperation of the defendant's circumstances against her. If an already desperate person is lucky enough to happen upon a heated, sanitary abandoned building, then a necessity defense may attach, but if the best abandoned building one can find is unheated, then one would be denied the defense of necessity, solely by virtue of that further piece of ill luck. The necessity defense should instead require only significant enhancement, or the greatest practical enhancement, in one's chances through the otherwise illegal act.

In general, however, our starvation and homelessness cases commonly pose the problems of weighing harms and benefits in reasonably manageable forms. Even people who are well off are usually willing to concede that the threats of starvation, severe malnutrition, or homelessness, on one occasion or chronically, are serious threats. Whatever the philosophical problems of commensurability, most people do not object to the idea that saving a life is somehow worth breaking into a vending machine.

Consider, for example, that we would not want the police to prevent all crimes for which only a "failed" or defective necessity defense could be offered. Suppose we know that someone's desperate hunger is entirely their own fault, and that they have foolishly bypassed legal sources of food. Presumably the courts would deny a necessity defense in such a case, but would be horrified by the thought of the police's preventing the defendant's crime, resulting in her death by starvation.

We need not concern ourselves unduly with the generality of the consequences to be considered. No doubt it would be a bad thing if a thousand starving persons stole one loaf of bread each. But an appropriate necessity defense limits its own impact on the institution of property rights and the rule of law. Much of the impact in such a case would really stem from the alterable fact that a thousand persons are starving or homeless, regardless of how they cope with their condition. And if we insist on assuming a thousand necessitous property crimes against many property owners, we must therefore also assume and consider a thousand persons who are thereby better off with respect to life and health. After all, as we have argued above, the number of people who will seek to take improper advantage of a necessity defense is likely to either be low or judicially controllable, for practical reasons.

We have admitted that, for example, a homeless person might enter an abandoned building and still contract influenza or some other disease, and perhaps die as a result. But such possibilities certainly do not limit or disqualify other defenses. Consider the case of someone who is physically attacked and responds with active self-defense. To put the matter as simply as possible, does the law factor in how likely the self-defense is to be effective, or how effective or ineffective it turned out to be, before accepting or rejecting the victim's plea of self-defense?

Consider, for example, an attacker who threatens to break the victim's arm, and who, over the victim's resistance, predictably succeeds in doing exactly that. Suppose that the attacker is a large male and that the victim is an unarmed female who is capable of injuring the attacking male, and who does so, but who is equally clearly unable, through her attempted self-defense, to prevent the attacker from precisely carrying out his threat.

Let us ask simply whether a jury would, in such a case, reasonably reject a claim of self-defense for the victim's injuring the attacker. We have assumed that the victim could not reasonably, through her self-defense, have expected to reduce the effect of the attacker's injury on her. We may also assume that resisting ineffectively may have both positive and negative psychological effects for the victim. Would a reasonable jury on that basis then dismiss the self-defense claim, on the theory that the victim was merely acting vainly, recklessly, or vindictively? Surely not. But we should expect some similar latitude to be extended to the homeless, for example. An otherwise appropriate necessity defense in a case of breaking into an abandoned building should not be lost if, for example, the defendant foreseeably became seriously ill despite obtaining shelter from the elements.

There remain, however, further general elements of the necessity defense to consider. It is, in particular, commonly assumed that for a necessity defense to be valid, the conduct of the defendant must not fall within circumstances in which the legislature has clearly intended to prohibit the defense of necessity. As a matter of morality or sound public policy, for example, a legislature might rule out the defense of necessity in any case in which the defendant has killed some innocent person. Thus one must not, even to avoid starvation, shoot some unoffending person. This legislative declaration thus might supplement or clarify what we have discussed above as the "proportionality" of the defendant's act.

We have no objection to applying this general element to the cases of concern to us. We may assume, for example, that even in matters of life and death, the death need not be that of some innocent stranger to the defendant. And we have already discussed the possibility of judicially or legislatively barring, even for necessitous defendants, burglarizing occupied residences for the sake of obtaining food or housing. In principle there is nothing to stop a legislature from clearly barring any and all uses of a necessity defense by the desperate. In that event, our defendants would of course not be able to show all the required elements of necessity. But this, by itself, would hardly amount to an intellectually satisfying refutation of the necessity defense. We would still want to know why, in light of the relevant moral and policy considerations, the legislature prohibited all use by the desperate of a necessity defense.

Let us devote a moment to a final possible general element of a necessity defense. Some courts have required that the danger in which the necessitous defendant finds herself be a danger that is easily recognized by the average person. Whatever one may think of this possible element on the merits, it hardly seems burdensome to those desperate for food or shelter. Food and shelter are plainly elemental needs that are readily recognized as such, abstractly and in particular cases, by ordinary persons. But the strict logic of limiting the defense to cases in which the danger is readily diagnosed by ordinary outsiders is questionable.

What, for example, if a defendant happens to know that she will become seriously ill within a few hours unless she eats several of the daisies available, as it turns out, only in a public park where picking flowers is banned? Can we say that an average person happening upon this scene would easily recognize the nature of the necessity? Presumably not. But why should this fact undermine the case for a necessity defense under these circumstances?

Once the peculiar needs and circumstances of the daisy consumer were explained to the average person, of course, such a bystander would likely be more sympathetic to the defendant's plight. Perhaps this is how such an element is really intended to be understood. If an average person can easily grasp the necessity after the circumstances and the necessity are explained, the element would then be met.

Such an interpretation of this element would hardly jeopardize the interests of the starving, malnourished, and homeless. An explanation of the likely effects of a prolonged failure to consume food should not be necessary. Interpreted in this way, the element seems neither demanding nor, frankly, crucial. Perhaps it is best understood, along with other curious or not strictly relevant restrictions on the necessity defense, as one more device to prevent expanding the scope of the necessity defense in practice beyond judicially comfortable bounds.

After all, necessity is in any event unlikely to be determined solely by the defendant's own perhaps subjective or irrational judgment. A defendant who believes she will shortly die of malnutrition unless she consumes a number of Cartier's uncut diamonds is delusional, not necessitous. A court can simply find no necessity in such a case, without inquiring whether a sense of any necessity could be conveyed easily to an average person. This element may nonetheless reflect some lingering fear of an irrational defendant pleading a sincerely believed, if preposterous, necessity. But this awkward driving of redundant nails into the coffin of an overextended necessity defense is no less redundant for being well intended.

We should remember that the idea of an insanity defense seems, in principle, vulnerable to gross abuse and overextension as well. Yet we do not, in practice, find juries acquitting significant numbers of plainly undeserving, or for that matter, apparently deserving, persons through an insanity defense. The threat of enormous numbers of criminal defendants, many with genuinely damaged psyches, successfully pleading insanity is in the abstract quite real. But the judicial system imposes a number of constraints on the pleading and proving of insanity, thereby avoiding substantial abuse.

Analogous possibilities exist with regard to a carefully considered necessity defense. And while some forms of legal insanity may be difficult to prevent or cure prior to the commission of some serious crime, homelessness is a problem more of moral and political priorities than of limits on our society's sheer technical capacity to provide minimal housing. This is not, again, to deny that some homeless persons have serious psychological or personal problems, or that for some homeless persons, merely providing a physical living space will not suffice. All we mean to suggest is that some cases of insanity are currently beyond even our theoretical grasp. We have no idea how, in theory, such persons might be cured. On the other hand, it is not lack of a theory of housing that prevents us from making significant progress in addressing the problems of the homeless.

Let us conclude, then, with a few theoretical observations about the idea of necessity. In particular, we must briefly contrast the idea of necessity with that of duress. Then we will consider whether necessity as a defense should, for our purposes, best be thought of as a matter of legally justifying the defendant's act, or as merely establishing a legally sufficient excuse for that act. Finally, we will with equal brevity address the relationship between the elements required for a necessity defense and the states of mind and circumstances that undermine criminal moral responsibility in the lives of the most deprived.

The legal defenses of necessity and duress are often linked. Quite frequently, they are treated by the courts as equivalent. Statutes and adjudicated cases often decline to draw any significant distinction between the two. Academic commentators often insist, on one ground or another, that a distinction should nevertheless be drawn. For some purposes the commentators may well be right. But in our context, we may say that the distinction is difficult to draw, or need not be drawn at all. In any event, there seems little real harm in referring as we have in this chapter merely to necessity, without reference to duress.

When an attempt is made to distinguish between necessity and duress, most commonly the distinction is said to depend on a basic distinction between the natural and the human, and in particular between natural threats and human threats to the defendant. If the idea of natural "threats" seems metaphorical, the distinction can be reformulated as one of the effects of natural circumstances and of human threats. If the idea of human threats, on the other hand, seems too narrow or dependent on intention, we might refer instead to necessitous circumstances that are brought about by human actors, whether threateningly or intentionally, or not.

Most of our cases of starvation, severe malnutrition, and homelessness do not necessarily involve any literal human threat, any intention that particular persons suffer, or any desire to coerce or manipulate the desperate into doing particular things for the benefit of any human. No person, group, or society in general need be thought of as holding the metaphorical gun of starvation or homelessness against the temple of the desperate in order to induce the desperate to do something favorable to the coercers. Most persons, certainly, may be merely indifferent to the plight of the desperate.

This does not mean, of course, that no groups profit, in any sense, from starvation or homelessness, whether they intend or appreciate such profit or not. And more important, the genuine necessitousness of the desperate and the existence of all the legal elements of necessity are not diminished even if no one intends that there be starvation and homelessness. By analogy, we might say that someone who is unintentionally locked in a room, or who is merely not released from the room, possesses no more physical freedom of movement than would a prison inmate. The necessity defense, as it were, logically requires no malice, deliberation, or identifiable constraining actors.

Certainly, though, our necessity cases take place in a social context, and to a substantial degree have social causes and possible social cures. But the degree to which this is so does not seem crucially relevant to the necessity defense. Whether we prefer in some cases to refer to duress instead of necessity can hardly be crucial for our purposes.

Consider, for purposes of illustration, a continuum of cases gradually becoming less purely "natural" and more purely social. Let us take the case of someone who will be injured in a fire unless she illegally enters a shelter owned by another person. Of course, fires are of all sorts, and all fires today imply some mixture of causes both natural and social. But different fires may have different social components. Perhaps the most purely natural fire might be caused by a lightning strike in a rarely visited forest. Of course, the environmentally attuned will recognize social components in even this situation. Next might be a fire obviously reflecting poor conservation policy, then a fire that reflects careless smoking of cigarettes. Some fires are deliberately set. Finally, one might start a fire precisely in order to kill a known intended victim, or in order to coerce that person into doing something to promote one's own interest.

These various sorts of fires clearly have different legal implications for many purposes. But for purposes of establishing a necessity defense, the differences simply do not seem significant. The issue of "proportionality" or the balancing of interests may, but need not, vary. Someone who, under the circumstances, is endangered by one of the fires may be equally endangered by any of the other fires. Smoke inhalation or burning seem distinctly undesirable outcomes even in the less clearly social cases, however much more reprehensible we may find deliberately burning a victim.

Nor does there seem any reason to refer to illegally obtaining shelter in the relatively "natural" cases as a matter of duress, but to switch at some not entirely obvious point to the idea of necessity when the circumstances of the fire are more clearly social, personal, or intentional. Where, precisely, should the switch from a duress defense to a necessity defense be made? And why, for our purposes, should it matter? Anyone who wishes to rewrite the argument of this chapter in terms of duress is welcome to undertake that not particularly taxing, if also not particularly rewarding, task.

Does it matter, though, whether we think of necessity as a matter of whether the defendant's act was fully justified, or as legally excusable but not justified? The distinction between justification and excuse, generally or in necessity cases, is not always clear or judicially respected. But some sort of theoretical difference can be drawn. We might, for example, say that what the necessitous defendant did was legally justified if it was the choice that maximized the values recognized by the law in such cases, or if it was the overall right thing to do.

One can thus say that illegally entering a city park after closing hours in order to save a drowning child was in this sense legally justified. But a necessity defense, on some theories, may not always involve this degree of ringing legal endorsement. We can imagine recognizing a necessity defense in the case of persons of whom we are not quite willing to say that they did the right or best thing under the circumstances. We may consider a defendant's act not justifiable in this strong sense, but still excusable, which in this sense would mean something like legally understandable or legally forgivable under the circumstances.

To accept a necessity defense might, for example, mean only that the court or jurors have concluded that had they themselves, or a hypothetical reasonable person, found themselves in something like the defendant's circumstances, with only the defendant's resources available, they too would probably have acted as the defendant did. In effect, the court or jury would be concluding that while the defendant's conduct was not legally justified in the strong sense, they or a reasonable person would likely have done no better than the defendant. In such a case, the court or jury is not fully endorsing the defendant's conduct, but instead officially admitting that it is in no position, without hypocrisy, to legally condemn what the defendant has done.

Or so some theorists of necessity might argue. For our purposes, it does not greatly matter whether we think of the necessity defense as involving full justification or mere excuse, or some interesting hybrid. It may be, admittedly, that some problems force us to choose between the two approaches. Consider, for example, a genuinely necessitous theft of a loaf of bread, where the shop owner happens to notice the theft in progress and resists the theft, perhaps causing a sprained ankle for the bread thief.

Some might argue that the liability of the shop owner for the thief's sprained ankle may actually depend on whether the court applies a justification or an excuse theory of the necessity defense. A legally justified act by the bread thief may have more legally recognized moral or social value than a merely legally excused act. An argument could therefore be made that a justified bread theft may have a claim not to be physically interfered with that is not shared by a merely excused bread theft.

It is difficult to believe, however, that any such possible distinction should govern the shop owner's liability. No doubt it is fair and reasonable to expect shop owners to exercise reasonable restraint in the defense of their property. An unarmed bread thief should not be subjected to a fusillade of gunfire from the shop owner. But it is unrealistic and unreasonable to expect shop owners to calibrate their resistance to shoplifters in accordance with a distinction between full justification and mere excuse. Shop owners cannot be expected to quickly and accurately determine even whether a theft is genuinely necessitous or not, let alone the theft's more precise overall moral status.

Even if, for example, potentially necessitous bread thieves were issued bright colored jerseys to indicate their status, shopkeepers could reasonably become skeptical in particular cases. Suppose the bread thief insists first on a second loaf, and then a toothbrush, and then several Cornish game hens, some cheese doodles, a gallon of premium ice cream, a case of German beer, and so on. Should the official jersey immunize even the most elaborate such shopping trip from any physical resistance by the shop owner? The distinction between justified and merely excused conduct is murky enough at the theoretical and judicial levels. The law should certainly not call on shopkeepers to make such determinations on the spot.

Finally, then, let us clarify the relationship between necessity and general moral responsibility. We have assumed that it is possible for persons who commit otherwise criminal acts out of necessity to nevertheless bear moral responsibility for their acts. How common this will be of course depends on the breadth or narrowness of one's theory of what is required for such responsibility. For the sake of the argument, we have at least held open the possibility of morally responsible necessitousness.

To help clarify this possibility, we might think of genuine necessitousness as in some cases presenting an easy choice between two alternatives. The ease of the choice, on such a theory, reflects the fact that one alternative quite clearly promotes the chooser's interests and preferences less than the other. Suppose, by way of analogy, that one were faced with a choice between six lashes with a rattan cane or four identical lashes. In describing one's preference for the latter option, one might well talk in terms of the ease and unstrained character of the decision-making process. One would not necessarily report that one found oneself helplessly drawn to the latter choice, as though one's ability to deliberate or choose were being bypassed or overwhelmed by one's brute desires or by the sheer force of circumstances.

Some artists and philosophers may be inclined to think of necessity as overwhelming the normal processes of decision making, rather than as posing a perhaps easy choice between two options, one of which may be clearly less appealing than the other. We should certainly grant that many cases of genuine necessity may pose difficult, even agonizing choice problems. Some persons would literally rather die than involve themselves in the shame and disgrace of theft and criminal prosecution. Some persons would view the choice, all things considered, between less adequate but legal housing and far more adequate but illegal housing as extremely difficult.

But one may bear full moral responsibility for some choices that seem "dictated" by one's moral principles, even where one cannot imagine doing otherwise. We may freely endorse the moral principles doing the "dictating." And it is also possible to bear full moral responsibility for a choice that is, subjectively, extremely difficult. Central cases of bearing full moral responsibility will often involve complex, difficult, subtle decisions agonized over at some length by the decision maker. Some cases of military strategy choice are surely like this. Some difficult choices made under necessitous circumstances may involve the full moral responsibility of otherwise competent decision makers.

There are, however, some necessity defense cases where the will of the defendant was overwhelmed or made irrelevant by the circumstances. A homeless person may, for example, have been morally responsible for how exhausted she is at a particular time. But if she finds herself, for whatever reason, on public property in a state of extreme exhaustion, her will may simply be overborne after some point. It is not within the capacities of mortals to postpone sleep, until one has found a legal sleeping place. If sleep is under these circumstances involuntary, we may then link involuntary conduct to the necessity defense. But being simply unable to any longer keep awake is not, as we have seen in some detail, the core of all housing necessity cases.

c o n c l u s i o n

At the beginning of this book, we met a person who lived, disastrously, in a temporarily broken trash compactor. This book has tried to redeem some legal space for such persons.

It is difficult to be entirely satisfied with current thinking about poverty, obligation, and responsibility. Wide ranges of people accused of crime and immorality deny their responsibility on various ingenious grounds. Everyone seems to have an excuse for every behavior. Naturally, the citizenry eventually wearies of this. Many citizens and officials take nearly universal obligation and responsibility for granted. This sometimes results in what their critics commonly refer to as blaming the victim. Of course, one can in some sense be a victim yet still richly deserve blame. But not always. If a victim's world is sufficiently grimly different from our own, blaming the victim neither confers nor recognizes dignity. Our judgments as to consent and culpability of the most deprived must take that deprivation into proper account.

It is, however, also important to recognize the dangers of various sorts of determinism. Harsh economic circumstances do not exceptionlessly dictate the direction of one's life. A few persons may be able to escape from even the most daunting prison. Environmental determinism of a rigid, universal, crudely reductive sort risks obscuring the absolute value of persons. This result would transform a well-intentioned, compassionate public policy impulse into a long-term disaster. Similar risks follow upon some broader forms of philosophical determinism. We can reject crude environmental determinism without holding the most deprived to unreasonable standards.

Some of our best contemporary thinkers decline to hold the most deprived responsible only because they hold no one responsible for anything. Perhaps we may, for genetic or cultural reasons, be merely unable to surrender the illusion of responsibility. Or perhaps we can actually wring all the traditional metaphysics out of the idea of responsibility, and use only a thin, residual version of it. This new, minimalist idea of responsibility might be used as an instrument to discourage undesired behavior, or to redress what we take to be imbalances in the scales of life's fortunes. The attractions of such an approach are obvious; its risks are less obvious and, as we have briefly noted above, enormous. Crucial ideas of moral responsibility cannot be disposed of without ultimately impeaching the notion of human dignity in particular and any objectivity or reality of morals in general.

Many leading academics are quite willing to abandon all objectivity of morals. We will say no more about the merits of this issue.[1] Let us instead close by speculating briefly about the genealogy of morals, and particularly about the process of progressive thought's abandonment of the idea of moral objectivity.

Anything the progressive wishes to say can easily be said within the language of moral objectivity. Moral objectivity is, at the very least, fully compatible with any degree of emphasis one cares to place on freedom, history, equality, pluralism, culture and society, tolerance, diversity, or group identity. Of course, oppressed groups have always found entrenched ideas of objectivity stacked against them. This means only that what dominant groups claim to be objectively true may not be objectively true. We have argued that despite the historical oppression of the poor in the name of alleged objective moral values, and the continuing abuse of the idea of objective moral principle today, abandoning moral objectivity itself as a regulative ideal would likely be disastrous for the poor over the long term.

Progressives may be led to reject any worries about abandoning the pursuit of moral objectivity by making a virtue of alleged necessity. If there really are no objective moral principles, why not assume, delightfully, that this unavoidable state of affairs really promotes the interests of the politically weak? An important role in this line of thought is being played, one suspects, by some traditional elements in progressive thought. First, much progressive thought has emphasized science and history, as opposed to moral argument. Even if science is thought to require objectivity, the objectivity of morals is thus of lesser concern. And second, progressive thought has historically emphasized, as the very term would suggest, the idea of progress and the inevitability of progress. In particular, progress was thought to take the form of the inevitable victory of the oppressed.

To the extent that progressive thought still de-emphasizes moral concepts and assumes progress in the form of the inevitable triumph of the poor, we can better understand why progressives are currently willing to dispense even with the ideal itself of moral objectivity. The problem, however, is this: much contemporary progressive thought does not believe in the ideal of scientific objectivity or the idea of progress, let alone the inevitability of progress.

If our genetic makeup or some technical imperative of postmodern civilization impelled us to properly address the circumstances of the most deprived, progressives might reasonably abandon moral objectivity. But this optimism seems unwarranted. The abuse of the idea of moral objectivity has obviously injured the poor, but would abandoning human dignity and any other interest in moral objectivity release unprecedented flows of empathy, compassion, solidarity, and sacrifice? Self-sacrifice, with no objective reason therefor, may have some passing appeal as a vaguely romantic pose. But this is unlikely to be particularly stable or popular over the long term.

Let us take a particular example that should be of concern in a post-industrial, information age society. We may have entered an era in which the actual employment marketplace never offers employment at a meaningful wage to large numbers of persons. This state of affairs may well be optimal for the relatively well off. Meaningful employment for more persons would require that the well off engage in conscious sacrifice on a continuing basis. How eager should progressives be to abandon objective moral argument, and to instead rely on the quite limited ability of the poor to threaten the system with disruption? This would not seem an appealing future for the contemporary poor.

Those genuinely concerned about the well-being of the least well off need not doubt that pretenses to moral objectivity have always been used as, among other things, a weapon against the poor and disenfranchised. But it is equally important to remember that without a sincere aspiration to moral objectivity, prospects for the poor must be even worse.

n o t e s

Note to the Introduction

1. See Jonathan Kozol, Rachel and Her Children: Homeless Families in America 175 (1988).

Notes to Chapter 1

1. 350 F.2d 445 (D.C. Cir. 1965) (involving credit terms and a security arrangement between the creditor and a debtor with seven children subsisting on a government check).

2. See Thomas Paine, Rights of Man 234-35 (Philip S. Foner ed., 1974).

3. Cass R. Sunstein, The Partial Constitution 155 (1993).

4. Peter Warr, Paul Jackson, and Michael Banks, Unemployment and Mental Health: Some British Studies, 44 J. Social Issues 47, 61 (1988).

5. See, e.g., R. George Wright, Reason and Obligation chs. 1-4 (1994).

6. See Thomas Aquinas, Summa Theologica II-II, question 66, article 7. See also id. at reply to objection 2. Of course, issues of nonviolence, public or private reimbursement, or penance may also play a role in Aquinas's scheme. See id. at question 66.

Notes to Chapter 2

1. Susan Wolf, Freedom Within Reason 140-41 (1990).

2. Id. at 144.

3. Id. at 117.

4. Gary Watson, Free Action and Free Will, 96 Mind 145, 152 (1987).

5. For further enlightenment, the reader is directed to Alex Kotlowitz, There Are No Children Here: The Story of Two Boys Growing Up in The Other America 239 (1991).

6. This description and other facts are taken from Singleton v. State, 465 So. 2d 432, 434-35 (Ala. Crim. App. 1983). See also Singleton v. State, 548 So. 2d 167 (Ala. 1989); Singleton v. Thigpen, 488 U.S. 1019 (1989).

7. See People v. Harris, 28 Cal. 3d 935, 944-45, 623 P.2d 240, 244, 171 Cal. Rptr. 679, 683 (1981). The later procedural history of this case is, incidentally, the stuff of legends and law review articles.

8. Arthur Conan Doyle, The Final Problem, in Sherlock Holmes: The Complete Novels and Stories Vol. 1 642, 645 (1892; Bantam ed., 1986).

9. United States v. Manzella, 791 F.2d 1263, 1269 (7th Cir. 1986).

10. United States v. Carter, 436 F.2d 200, 210 (D.C. Cir. 1970) (Bazelon, C. J., concurring).

11. Eddings v. State, 616 P.2d 1159, 1170 (Okla. Crim. App. 1980), rev'd, 455 U.S. 104 (1982).

12. Galen Strawson, Freedom and Belief 219 n. 22 (1986).

Notes to Chapter 3

1. Kathryn M. Grossman, Hugo's Romantic Sublime: Beyond Chaos and the Conventions in Les Misérables, 60 Philological Q. 471, 474 (1981).

2. Daniel H. Lowenstein, The Failure of the Act: Conceptions of Law in The Merchant of Venice, Bleak House, Les Miserables, and Richard Weisberg's Poethics, 15 Cardozo L. Rev. 1139, 1222 (1994).

3. See the opinion of Tatting, J., in Lon L. Fuller, The Case of the Speluncean Explorers, 62 Harv. L. Rev. 616, 629-30 (1949).

4. Victor Hugo, Les Miserables 83, trans. Lee Fahnestock and Norman MacAfee (1862; Signet ed., 1987).

5. See Francis S. Heck, The Loaf of Bread in Les Miserables and in Zola's Travail, 24 Romance Notes 254 (1984). For the incident of Nanet's bread theft itself, see Emile Zola, Work 25-28, trans. Ernest A. Vizetelly (1925).

6. See Charles Dickens, The Adventures of Oliver Twist 13 (1838; Oxford Univ. Press ed., 1987).

7. State v. Moe, 174 Wash. 303, 24 P.2d 638 (1933).

8. 24 P.2d at 640.

9. Id.

10. See, e.g., Michael M. Burns, Responding to Beggars, 1991 Wis. L.

Rev. 1101, 1103; Nancy A. Millich, Compassion Fatigue and the First Amendment: Are the Homeless Constitutional Castaways?, 27 U. Cal. Davis L. Rev. 255, 265 (1994).

11. For discussion, in order, of these issues, see Loper v. New York City Police Dep't, 999 F.2d 699 (2d Cir. 1993); Young v. New York City Transit Auth., 903 F.2d 146 (2d Cir.), cert. denied, 498 U.S. 984 (1990); Roulette v. City of Seattle, 850 F. Supp. 1442 (W.D. Wash. 1994); Chad v. City of Fort Lauderdale, 861 F. Supp. 1057 (S.D. Fla. 1994).

12. See, e.g., Allan Hutchinson, *Les Misérables* Redux: Law and the Poor, 2 S. Cal. Interdisciplinary L. J. 199, 205 (1993) (citing a figure of 500,000 people); Harry Simon, Towns without Pity: A Constitutional and Historical Analysis of Official Efforts to Drive Homeless Persons from American Cities, 66 Tul. L. Rev. 631, 646-47 (1992) (citing a worsening figure of 3,000,000 persons); Jeremy Waldron, Homelessness and the Issue of Freedom, 39 UCLA L. Rev. 295, 299 (1991)(citing a range of 250,000 to three million persons). Of course, these estimates need not be inconsistent, depending on the definitions and measures chosen.

13. For a somewhat more vivid depiction, see Alice S. Baum and Donald W. Burns, A Nation in Denial: The Truth about Homelessness ch. 4, at 56-73 (1993).

14. Lindsey v. Normet, 405 U.S. 56, 74 (1972).

15. See Tobe v. City of Santa Ana, 27 Cal. App. 4th 1209, 1212, 27 Cal. Rptr. 2d 386, 387 (1994), rev'd, 9 Cal. 4th 1069, 892 P.2d 1145, 40 Cal. Rptr. 2d 402 (1995).

16. See Paulino v. Wright, 620 N.Y.S.2d 363 (App. Div. 1994), leave to appeal dismissed, 85 N.Y.2d 858, 648 N.E.2d 795, 624 N.Y.S.2d 375 (1995).

17. See Pottinger v. City of Miami, 810 F. Supp. 1551 (S.D. Fla. 1992), remanded for limited purposes, 40 F.3d 1155 (11th Cir. 1994).

18. Johnson v. City of Dallas, 860 F. Supp. 344, 350 (N.D. Tex. 1994).

19. 1971 L.R.—Ch. 734 (Ch. App. 1971).

20. See Regina v. Dudley and Stephens, 14 Q.B.D. 273 (1884).

21. 1971 L.R.—Ch. at 744.

Note to the Conclusion

1. For further discussion, see R. George Wright, Reason and Obligation ch. 5 (1994).

b i b l i o g r a p h y

Alexander, Larry. Inculpatory and Exculpatory Mistakes and the Fact/Law Distinction: An Essay in Memory of Myke Bayles. 12 Law and Phil. 33 (1993).

_____. Law and Exclusionary Reasons. 18 Phil. Topics 5 (1990).

Allen, Francis A. Criminal Justice, Legal Values and the Rehabilitative Ideal. In Theories of Punishment 317, ed. Stanley E. Grupp.

Allison, Henry E. Kant's Theory of Freedom. 1990.

_____. Book Review. 102 Ethics 655 (1992).

Amar, Akhil Reed. Forty Acres and a Mule: A Republican Theory of Minimal Entitlements. 23 Harv. J. L. and Pub. Pol'y 37 (1990).

Amezquita v. Colon, 518 F.2d 8 (1st Cir. 1975), cert. denied, 424 U.S. 916 (1976).

Anderson, Elijah. Streetwise: Race, Class, and Change in an Urban Community. 1990.

_____. Neighborhood Effects on Teenage Pregnancy. In The Urban Underclass 375, ed. Christopher Jencks and Paul E. Peterson. 1990.

Anderson, Susan L. A Picture of the Self Which Supports Moral Responsibility. 74 Monist 43 (1991).

Andre, Judith. Nagel, Williams, and Moral Luck. 43 Analysis 202 (1983).

Arenella, Peter. Convicting the Morally Blameless: Reassessing the Relationship between Legal and Moral Accountability. 39 UCLA L. Rev. 1511 (1992).

Arkes, Hadley. First Things. 1986.

Arneson, Richard J. Meaningful Work and Market Socialism. 97 Ethics 517 (1987).

_____. The Principle of Fairness and Free Rider Problems. 92 Ethics 616 (1982).

Audi, Robert. Moral Responsibility, Freedom, and Compulsion. 11 Am. Phil. Q. 1 (1974).

_____. Responsible Action and Virtuous Character. 101 Ethics 304 (1991).

Augustine, Saint. On Free Choice of the Will, trans. Anna S. Benjamin and L. H. Hackstaff. 1964.

Auletta, Ken. The Underclass. 1983.

Aune, Bruce. Kant's Theory of Morals. 1979.

Backer, Larry Catá. Of Handouts and Worthless Promises: Understanding the Conceptual Limitations of American Systems of Poor Relief. 34 B.C. L. Rev. 997 (1993).

Balkin, J. M. The Rhetoric of Responsibility. 76 Va. L. Rev. 197 (1990).

Bandes, Susan. The Negative Constitution: A Critique. 88 Mich. L. Rev. 2271 (1990).

Bank of Columbia v. Okeley, 17 U.S. (4 Wheat.) 235 (1819).

Barry, Brian. Theories of Justice. 1989.

Baum, Alice S., and Donald W. Burns. A Nation in Denial: The Truth about Homelessness. 1993.

Baxter, Donald L. M. Free Choice. 67 Australasian J. Phil. 12 (1989).

Bayles, Michael D. Character, Purpose, and Criminal Responsibility. 1 Law and Phil. 5 (1982).

_____. Reconceptualizing Necessity and Duress. 33 Wayne L. Rev. 1191 (1987).

Bazelon, David L. Questioning Authority. 1988.

Beard, Charles A. An Economic Interpretation of the Constitution of the United States. 1919.

Bell v. State, 885 S.W.2d 282 (Tex. Crim. Ct. App. 1994).

Benditt, Theodore M. Rights. 1982.

Benn, Stanley I. A Theory of Freedom. 1988.

Bennett, Susan D. "No Relief But upon the Terms of Coming into the House": Controlled Spaces, Invisible Disentitlements, and Homelessness in an Urban Shelter System. 104 Yale L. J. 2157 (1995).

Benson, Paul. Book Review. 101 Mind 364 (1992).

Benson v. Cady, 761 F.2d 335 (7th Cir.), cert. denied, 470 U.S. 1052 (1985).

Beran, Harry. The Consent Theory of Political Obligation. 1987.

Berger, Fred. Gratitude. 85 Ethics 298 (1975).

Berlin, Isaiah. Two Concepts of Liberty. In Four Essays on Liberty 118. 1968.

Bernstein, Richard J. Beyond Objectivism and Relativism: Science, Hermeneutics, and Praxis. 1983.

Berofsky, Bernard. Freedom from Necessity. 1987.

_____. Book Review. 89 J. Phil. 202 (1992).

_____. On the Absolute Freedom of the Will. 29 Am. Phil. Q. 279 (1992).

Bickenbach, Jerome E. The Defence of Necessity. 13 Can. J. Phil. 79 (1983).

Bitensky, Susan H. Theoretical Foundations for a Right to Education under the U.S. Constitution: A Beginning to the End of the National Education Crisis. 86 Nw. U. L. Rev. 550 (1992).

Black, Charles L. Further Reflections on the Constitutional Justice of Livelihood. 86 Colum. L. Rev. 1103 (1986).

Blau, Joel. The Visible Poor: Homelessness in the United States. 1992.

Bluestone, Barry, and Bennett Harrison. The Deindustrialization of America: Plant Closings, Community Abandonment, and the Dismantling of Basic Industry. 1982.

Board of Educ. v. Nyquist, 57 N.Y.2d 27, 439 N.E.2d 359, 453 N.Y.S.2d 643 (1982), appeal dismissed, 459 U.S. 1139 (1983).

Board of Educ. v. Walter, 58 Ohio St. 2d 368, 390 N.E.2d 813 (1979), cert. denied, 444 U.S. 1015 (1980).

Board of Regents v. Roth, 408 U.S. 564, 588 (1972) (Marshall, J., dissenting).

Boddie v. Connecticut, 401 U.S. 371 (1971).

Bodenheimer, Edgar. Philosophy of Responsibility. 1980.

Boldt, Richard C. The Construction of Responsibility in the Criminal Law. 140 U. Pa. L. Rev. 2245 (1992).

Bourke, Vernon. Review of John Finnis' Natural Law and Natural Rights. 26 Am. J. Juris. 243 (1981).

Boyde v. California, 494 U.S. 370 (1990) (Marshall, J., dissenting).

Bradley, F. H. Ethical Studies. 2d ed. 1927.

Braybrooke, David. Meeting Needs. 1987.

Brest, Paul. Further beyond the Republican Revival: Toward Radical Republicanism. 97 Yale L. J. 1623 (1988).

Brilmayer, Lea. Consent, Contract, and Territory. 74 Minn. L. Rev. 1 (1989).

Brock, Gillian. Braybrooke on Needs. 104 Ethics 811 (1994).

Browne, Brynmor. A Solution to the Problem of Moral Luck. 42 Phil. Q. 345 (1992).

Brudner, Alan. A Theory of Necessity. 7 Ox. J. Legal Stud. 339 (1987).

Buchanan, James M. The Limits of Liberty: Between Anarchy and Leviathan. 1975.

Buchanan, James M., and Loren Lomasky. The Matrix of Contractarian Justice. In Liberty and Equality, ed. Ellen Frankel Paul et al. 1985.

Buckley v. Valeo, 424 U.S. 1 (1976).

Bullock v. Whiteman, 254 Kan. 177, 865 P.2d 197 (1993).

Burns, Michael M. Responding to Beggars. 1991 Wis. L. Rev. 1101.

Calder v. Bull, 3 U.S. (3 Dall.) 386, 388 (1798) (Chase, J.).

Calhoun, Cheshire. Responsibility and Reproach. 99 Ethics 389 (1989).

California Grocers Ass'n v. Bank of America, 22 Cal. App. 4th 205, 27 Cal. Rptr. 2d 396 (1994).

California v. Brown, 479 U.S. 538 (1987) (O'Connor, J., concurring).

Campbell, C. A. In Defence of Free Will. 1967.

Card, Claudia. Gratitude and Obligation. 25 Am. Phil. Q. 115 (1988).

Carr, Craig L. On Being Free to Choose. 17 J. Value Inquiry 203 (1983).

Carrier, L. S. Free Will and Intentional Action. 16 Philosophia 355 (1986).

Castro v. People, 346 P.2d 1020 (Colo. 1959) (en banc).

Chad v. City of Fort Lauderdale, 861 F. Supp. 1057 (S.D. Fla. 1994).

Charny, David. Hypothetical Bargains: The Normative Structure of Contract. 89 Mich. L. Rev. 1815 (1991).

Chemerinsky, Erwin. Making the Case for a Constitutional Right to Minimum Entitlements. 44 Mercer L. Rev. 525 (1993).

Chisholm, Roderick M. "He Could Have Done Otherwise." 64 J. Phil. 409 (1967).

Chisholm v. Georgia, 2 U.S. (2 Dall.) 419, 455 (1793) (Wilson, J.).

Church v. City of Huntsville, 30 F.3d 1332 (11th Cir. 1994).

Clarke, Randolph. Deliberation and Beliefs about One's Abilities. 73 Pac. Phil. Q. 101 (1992).

_____. Freedom and Determinism. 36 Phil. Books 9 (1995).

_____. Free Will and the Conditions of Moral Responsibility. 66 Phil. Stud. 53 (1992).

_____. Toward a Credible Agent-Causal Account of Free Will. 27 Nous 191 (1993).

Clowes v. Serrano, 432 U.S. 907 (1977).

Coll, Steve. Economic Change, Social Upheaval: Governments Cutting Welfare Benefits, Selling State-Run Firms. Washington Post, Aug. 7, 1994, at A1 (final ed.).

Collin v. Smith, 578 F.2d 1197 (7th Cir.), cert. denied, 439 U.S. 916 (1978).

Conde, Michelle R. Comment, Necessity Defined: A New Role in the Criminal Defense. 29 UCLA L. Rev. 409 (1981).

Constitutions of the World, ed. Albert P. Blaustein and Gisbert H. Flanz. 1994.

Cullen, Bernard. The Right to Work. In Moral Philosophy and Contemporary Problems 165, ed. J. D. G. Evans. 1987.

Currie, David P. Positive and Negative Constitutional Rights. 53 U. Chi. L. Rev. 864 (1986).

Dahl, Norman O. "Ought" and Blameworthiness. 64 J. Phil. 418 (1967).

Dandridge v. Williams, 397 U.S. 471 (1970).

Dawson's Lessee v. Godfrey, 8 U.S. (4 Cranch) 321 (1808).

Days, Drew S.III. Civil Rights at the Crossroads. 1 Temple Pol. and Civ. Rts. L. Rev. 29 (1992).

DeGeorge, Richard T. The Right to Work: Law and Ideology. 19 Val. U. L. Rev. 15 (1984).

de Jesus Benavides v. Santos, 883 F.2d 385 (5th Cir. 1989).

Delgado, Richard. "Rotten Social Background": Should the Criminal Law Recognize a Defense of Severe Environmental Deprivation? 3 Law and Ineq. J. 9 (1985).

Deloria, Vine, Jr., and Clifford M. Lytle. American Indians, American Justice. 1983.

de Marneffe, Peter. Contractualism, Liberty, and Democracy. 104 Ethics 764 (1994).

Dennett, Daniel C. Elbow Room. 1984.

DeShaney v. Winnebago County, 489 U.S. 189 (1989).

Dickens, Charles. The Adventures of Oliver Twist. 1838; Oxford Univ. Press ed., 1987.

DiUlio, John J., Jr. The Impact of Inner City Crime. 96 Pub. Interest 28 (1989).

Dooley, David, and Ralph Catalano. Recent Research on the Psychological Effects of Unemployment. 44 J. Social Issues 1 (1988).

Double, Richard. The Non-Reality of Free Will. 1991.

_____. Book Review. 101 Mind 198 (1993).

Doyle, Arthur Conan. The Final Problem. In Sherlock Holmes: The Complete Novels and Stories. 1892; Bantam ed., 1986.

Dred Scott v. Sanford, 60 U.S. (19 How.) 393 (1856).

Dressler, Joshua. The Exegesis of the Law of Duress: Justifying the Excuse and Searching for Its Proper Limits. 62 S. Cal. L. Rev. 1331 (1989).

_____. Foreword: Justifications and Excuses: A Brief Review of the Concepts and the Literature. 33 Wayne L. Rev. 1155 (1987).

Duff, R. A. Intention, Agency, and Criminal Liability: Philosophy of Action and the Criminal Law. 1990.

_____. Trials and Punishment. 1986.

Dworkin, Gerald. Acting Freely. 4 Nous 367 (1970).

Eddings v. Oklahoma, 455 U.S. 104 (1982).

Eddings v. State, 616 P.2d 1159 (Okla. Crim. App. 1980), rev'd, 455

U.S. 104 (1982).

Edelman, Peter B. The Next Century of Our Constitution: Rethinking Our Duty to the Poor. 39 Hastings L. J. 1 (1987).

Edin, Kathryn. Surviving the Welfare System: How AFDC Recipients Make Ends Meet in Chicago. 38 Social Probs. 461 (1991).

Ellenburg, Stephen. Rousseau's Political Philosophy. 1976.

Ellis, George F. R. Before the Beginning. 1993.

Ellis v. Mckinnon Broadcasting Co., 18 Cal. App 4th 1796, 23 Cal. Rptr. 2d 80 (1993).

Ellsworth v. City of Racine, 774 F.2d 182 (7th Cir. 1985), cert. denied, 475 U.S. 1047 (1986).

Ellwood, David T. Poor Support: Poverty in the American Family. 1988.

Emerson, Ralph Waldo. Self-Reliance. In Selected Essays 175, ed. Larzer Ziff. 1841; reprint, 1982.

Engstrom, Stephen. Book Review, 102 Ethics 653 (1992).

Epstein, David F. The Political Theory of the Federalist. 1984.

_____. The Political Theory of the Constitution. In Confronting the Constitution 77, ed. Allan Bloom. 1990.

Estate of Gilmore v. Buckley, 787 F.2d 714 (1st Cir.), cert. denied, 479 U.S. 882 (1986).

Ewen, Lynda A. All God's Children Ain't Got Shoes: A Comparison of West Virginia and the Urban "Underclass." 13 Humanity and Soc'y 145 (1989).

Fallon, Richard H., Jr. Individual Rights and the Powers of Government. 27 Ga. L. Rev. 343 (1993).

Farnsworth, E. Allan. Contracts §§ 2.17-.28. 2d ed., 1990.

Feinberg, Joel. Doing and Deserving. 1970.

_____. Rights, Justice and the Bounds of Liberty. 1980.

Feldman, Stephen M. The Persistence of Power and the Struggle for Dialogic Standards in Postmodern Constitutional Jurisprudence: Michelman, Habermas, and Civic Republicanism. 81 Geo. L. J.

2243 (1993).

Fennell, Lee Anne. Interdependence and Choice in Distributive Justice: The Welfare Conundrum. 1994 Wis. L. Rev. 235.

Finan, John P., and John Ritson. Tortious Necessity: The Privileged Defense. 26 Akron L. Rev. 1 (1992).

Finkelstein, Clair O. Duress: A Philosophical Account of the Defense in Law. 37 Ariz. L. Rev. 251 (1995).

Finnis, John. Natural Law and Natural Rights. 1980.

_____. Natural Law and Legal Reasoning, in Natural Law Theory: Contemporary Essays 134, ed. Robert P. George. 1992.

_____. The Authority of Law in the Predicament of Contemporary Social Theory. 1 Notre Dame J. L., Ethics and Pub. Pol'y 115 (1984).

Fischer, John Martin. The Metaphysics of Free Will: An Essay on Control. 1994.

Fischer, John Martin, and Paul Hoffman. Alternative Possibilities: A Reply to Lamb. 91 J. Phil. 321 (1994).

Fischer, John Martin, and Mark Ravizza. Responsibility and Inevitability. 101 Ethics 258 (1991).

Flathman, Richard E. The Philosophy and Politics of Freedom. 1987.

_____. Political Obligation. 1972.

_____. The Practice of Rights. 1976.

Foley, Richard. Compatibilism. 87 Mind 421 (1978).

Forsyth County v. Nationalist Movement, 505 U.S. 123 (1992).

Foucha v. Louisiana, 504 U.S. 71 (1992).

Frankfurt, Harry G. Coercion and Moral Responsibility. In Essays on Freedom of Action 65, ed. Ted Honderich. 1973.

Freedman, Jonathan. From Cradle to Grave: The Human Face of Poverty in America. 1993.

Freeman, Samuel. Reason and Agreement in Social Contract Views. 19 Phil. and Pub. Aff. 122 (1990).

French, Peter A. Responsibility Matters. 1992.

Fried, Charles. Right and Wrong. 1978.

Fromm, Erich. Escape from Freedom. 1941.

Fuller, Lon L. The Case of the Speluncean Explorers. 62 Harv. L. Rev. 616 (1949).

Garcia-Mir v. Meese, 788 F.2d 1446 (11th Cir.), cert. denied, 479 U.S. 889 (1986).

Gauthier, David. Morals by Agreement (1986).

_____. Between Hobbes and Rawls, in Rationality, Justice and the Social Contract 24, ed. David Gauthier and Robert Sugden. 1993.

_____. Morality, Rational Choice, and Semantic Representation: A Reply to My Critics. In The New Social Contract: Essays on Gauthier 173, ed. Ellen Frankel Paul et al. 1988.

_____. Why Contractarianism? In Contractarianism and Rational Choice 15, ed. Peter Vallentyne. 1991.

Gerhardt, Michael J. The Ripple Effects of Slaughterhouse: A Critique of a Negative Rights View of the Constitution. 43 Vand. L. Rev. 409 (1990).

Gewirth, Alan. Reason and Morality. 1978.

_____. Why Rights Are Indispensable. 95 Mind 329 (1986).

Gilbert, Margaret. Agreement, Coercion, and Obligation. 103 Ethics 679 (1993).

_____. Group Membership and Political Obligation. 76 Monist 119 (1993).

Glendon, Mary Ann. Rights Talk: The Impoverishment of Political Discourse. 1991.

_____. Rights in Twentieth Century Constitutions. 59 U. Chi. L. Rev. 519 (1992).

Glover, Jonathan. Responsibility. 1970.

Goldberg v. Kelly, 397 U.S. 254 (1970).

Golding, Martin P. Foreword: Issues in Responsibility. 49 Law and Contemp. Probs. 1 (1986).

Goodin, Robert E. Protecting the Vulnerable. 1985.

_____. Reasons for Welfare. 1988.

Gorr, Michael. Toward a Theory of Coercion. 16 Can. J. Phil. 383 (1986).

Gosselin, Phillip. The Principle of Alternate Possibilities. 17 Can. J. Phil. 91 (1987).

Graham, George. Doing Something Intentionally and Moral Responsibility. 11 Can. J. Phil. 667 (1981).

Grano, Joseph D. Ascertaining the Truth. 77 Cornell L. Rev. 1061 (1992).

Gray, John N. On Negative and Positive Liberty. 28 Pol. Stud. 507 (1980).

Green, Leslie. The Authority of the State. 1990.

_____. Consent and Community. In On Political Obligation 89, ed. Paul Harris. 1990.

Greenawalt, Kent. Distinguishing Justifications from Excuses. 49 Law and Contemp. Probs. 89 (1986).

_____. Promise, Benefit and Need: Ties That Bind Us to the Law. 18 Ga. L. Rev. 727 (1984).

Greenspan, P.S. Unfreedom and Responsibility. In Responsibility, Character, and the Emotions 63, ed. Ferdinand Schoeman. 1987.

_____. Free Will and the Genome Project. 22 Phil. and Pub. Aff. 31 (1993).

Greenstone, J. David. Culture, Rationality, and the Underclass. In The Urban Underclass 399, ed. Christopher Jencks and Paul E. Peterson. 1990.

Gregor, Mary. Kant on Welfare Legislation. In Poverty, Justice, and the Law 49, ed. George R. Lucas, Jr. 1986.

Griffin, Stephen M. Review of Rex Martin, A System of Rights. 68 Tul. L. Rev. 1689 (1994).

Griffin v. United States, 447 A.2d 776 (D.C. Ct. App. 1982), cert. denied sub nom. Snyder v. United States, 461 U.S. 907 (1983).

Griggs v. Duke Power Co., 401 U.S. 424 (1971).

Grisez, Germain. The First Principle of Practical Reason: A Commentary on the Summa Theologica, 1-2, Question 94, Article 2. 10 Natural L. F. 168 (1965).

Grossman, Kathryn M. Hugo's Romantic Sublime: Beyond Chaos and the Conventions in *Les Miserables*. 60 Philological Q. 471 (1981).

Guyer, Paul. Book Review. 89 J. Phil. 99 (1992).

Habermas, Jurgen. The Philosophical Discourse of Modernity, trans. Frederick Lawrence. 1987.

_____. Discourse Ethics: Notes on a Program of Philosophical Justification. In The Communicative Ethics Controversy 60, ed. Seyla Benhabib and Fred Dallmayr. 1990.

Hacker, Andrew. Two Nations. 1992.

Hagen v. Utah, 114 S. Ct. 958 (1994) (Blackmun, J., dissenting).

Haksar, Vinit. Excuses and Voluntary Conduct. 96 Ethics 317 (1986).

Hamling v. United States, 418 U.S. 87 (1974).

Hampton, Jean. Hobbes and the Social Contract Tradition. 1986.

Handler, Joel F. Dependent People, the State, and the Modern/Postmodern Search for the Dialogic Community. 35 UCLA L. Rev. 999 (1988).

Harman, Gilbert. Libertarianism and Morality. In The Libertarian Reader 226, ed. Tibor R. Machan. 1982.

_____. Moral Relativism Defended. In Relativism: Cognitive and Moral 189, ed. Jack W. Meiland and Michael Krausz. 1982.

Harris, Angela P., and Marjorie M. Shultz. "A(nother) Critique of Pure Reason": Toward Civic Virtue in Legal Education. 45 Stan. L. Rev. 1773 (1990).

Harris, David. Justifying State Welfare. 1987.

Harris, Edward A. Fighting Philosophical Anarchism with Fairness: The Moral Claims of Law in the Liberal State. 92 Colum. L. Rev. 919 (1991).

_____. From Social Contract to Hypothetical Agreement: Consent and the Obligation to Obey the Law. 92 Colum. L. Rev. 651 (1992).

Hart, H. L. A. Punishment and Responsibility. 1968.

_____. Are There Any Natural Rights? 65 Phil. Rev. 175 (1955).

Hart, H. L A., and Tony Honore. Causation in the Law. 2d ed., 1985.

Heck, Francis S. The Loaf of Bread in *Les Miserables* and in Zola's *Travail*. 24 Romance Notes 254 (1984).

Herman, Barbara. The Practice of Moral Judgment. 1993.

Hill, Christopher S. Watsonian Freedom and Freedom of the Will. 62 Australasian J. Phil. 294 (1984).

Hill, John L. Note, Freedom, Determinism, and the Externalization of Responsibility in the Law: A Philosophical Analysis. 76 Geo. L. J. 2045 (1988).

Hill, Thomas E. Jr. Dignity and Practical Reason in Kant's Moral Theory. 1992.

Hirsch, Eric, and Peter Wood. Squatting in New York City: Justification and Strategy. 16 N.Y.U. Rev. L. and Soc. Change 605 (1987–88).

Hirschmann, Nancy. Rethinking Obligation: A Feminist Method for Political Theory. 1992.

Hittinger, Russell. A Critique of the New Natural Law Theory. 1987.

Hobbes, Thomas. Leviathan. Prometheus Books ed., 1988.

Hobhouse, Leonard T. Liberalism. 1964.

Hodgson, David. The Mind Matters: Consciousness and Choice in a Quantum World. 1991.

Homestead Act of 1862, ch. 75, 12 Stat. 392 (1862) (repealed 1976).

Honderich, Ted. A Theory of Determinism: The Mind, Neuroscience, and Life-Hopes. 1988.

Honore, Tony. A Theory of Coercion. 10 Oxford J. Legal Stud. 94 (1990).

Hope, Marjorie, and James Young. The Faces of Homelessness. 1986.

Horgan, Terence. "Could," Possible Worlds, and Moral Responsibility.

17 S. J. Phil. 345 (1979).

Horowitz, Donald L. Justification and Excuse in the Program of the Criminal Law. 49 Law and Contemp. Probs. 109 (1986).

Horton v. Meskill, 195 Conn. 24, 486 A.2d 1099 (1985).

Hospers, John. Libertarianism. 1971.

Hugo, Victor. Les Miserables, trans. Lee Fahnestock and Norman MacAfee. 1987.

Huigens, Kyron. Virtue and Inculpation. 108 Harv. L. Rev. 1423 (1995).

Hume, David. A. An Enquiry Concerning the Principles of Morals. Open Court ed., 1960.

_____. Treatise of Human Nature, ed. E. C. Mossner 1969.

Hurd, Heidi M. Challenging Authority. 100 Yale L. J. 1611 (1991).

Hutchinson, Allan C. Les Miserables Redux: Law and the Poor. 2 S. Cal. Interdisciplinary L. J. 199 (1993).

Illinois v. Allen, 397 U.S. 337 (1970) (opinion of Douglas, J.).

Jacobs, Lesley A. Rights and Deprivation. 1993.

Jahoda, Marie. Economic Recession and Mental Health: Some Conceptual Issues. 44 J. Social Issues 13 (1988).

Jencks, Christopher. The Homeless. 1994.

_____. Rethinking Social Policy. 1992.

Johnson v. City of Dallas, 860 F. Supp. 344 (N.D. Tex. 1994).

Johnson v. State, 439 A.2d 542 (Md. 1982).

Jordan, Jeff. Why Negative Rights Only? 29 S. J. Phil. 245 (1991).

Joyce v. City and County of San Francisco, 846 F. Supp. 843 (N.D. Cal. 1994).

Kane, Robert. Free Will and Moral Responsibility: A Review of Bruce N. Waller's Freedom Without Responsibility. 20 Behavior and Phil. 77 (1992).

Kant, Immanuel. Foundations of the Metaphysics of Morals. trans. Lewis White Beck. 1959.

Karst, Kenneth L. Citizenship, Race and Marginality, 30 Wm. and

Mary L. Rev. 1 (1988).

Kaus, Mickey. The End of Equality. 1993.

Kavka, Gregory S. Hobbesian Moral and Political Theory. 1986.

Kelman, Mark. Interpretive Construction in the Substantive Criminal Law. 33 Stan. L. Rev. 591 (1981).

Kenny, Anthony. The Metaphysics of Mind. 1989.

Kerruish, Valerie. Philosophical Retreat: A Criticism of John Finnis' Theory of Natural Law. 15 U. W. Aust. L. Rev. 224 (1983).

King v. United States, 372 F.2d 383 (D.C. Cir. 1966).

Klein, Martha. Determinism, Blameworthiness, and Deprivation. 1990.

Klosko, George. The Principle of Fairness and Political Obligation. 1992.

_____. Four Arguments against Political Obligation from Gratitude. 5 Pub. Aff. Q. 33 (1991).

_____. Political Obligation and the Natural Duties of Justice. 23 Phil. and Pub. Aff. 251 (1994).

_____. Presumptive Benefit, Fairness, and Political Obligation. 16 Phil. and Pub. Aff. 241 (1987).

Kotlowitz, Alex. There Are No Children Here: The Story of Two Boys Growing Up in The Other America. 1991.

Kozol, Jonathan. Rachel and Her Children: Homeless Families in America. 1988.

_____. Savage Inequalities. 1991.

Kristjánsson, Kristján. Social Freedom and the Test of Moral Responsibility. 103 Ethics 104 (1992).

LaFave, Wayne R., and Austin W. Scott, Jr. Criminal Law. 2d ed.,1986.

Lambert v. California, 355 U.S. 225 (1956).

Langbein, John H. Shaping the Eighteenth-Century Criminal Trial: A View from the Ryder Sources. 50 U. Chi. L. Rev. 1 (1983).

Larson, Arthur. The Law of Workmen's Compensation. 1993.

Lee v. New York City, 622 N.Y.S.2d 944 (App. Div. 1995).

Lelling, Andrew E. Eliminative Materialism, Neuroscience and the Criminal Law, 141 U. Pa. L. Rev. 1471 (1993).

Lemos, Ramon. Rousseau's Political Philosophy. 1977.

_____. Determinism and Political Freedom. 60 Personalist 101 (1979).

Levenbrook, Barbara B. Responsibility and the Normative Order Assumption. 49 Law and Contemp. Probs. 81 (1986).

Levin, Michael. Negative Liberty. In Liberty and Equality 84, ed. Ellen Frankel Paul et al. 1985.

Levitin, Joel H. Putting the Government on Trial: The Necessity Defense and Social Change. 33 Wayne L. Rev. 1221 (1987).

Lewis, C. S. The Humanitarian Theory of Punishment. In Theories of Punishment 301, ed. Stanley E. Grupp. 1971.

Lichtenberg, Judith. Subjectivism as Moral Weakness Projected. 33 Phil. Q. 378 (1983).

Liem, Ramsay, and Joan Huser Liem. Psychological Effects of Unemployment on Workers and Their Families. 44 J. Social Issues 87 (1988).

Lindgren, J. Ralph. Criminal Responsibility Reconsidered. 6 Law and Phil. 89 (1987).

Lindsey v. Normet, 405 U.S. 56 (1972).

Locke, John. The Second Treatise on Civil Government. Prometheus Books ed., 1986.

Lockett v. Ohio, 438 U.S. 586 (1978) (Burger, C.J., for the plurality).

Lockwood, Michael. Mind, Brain and the Quantum. 1989.

Loewenstein, Gaither. The New Underclass: A Contemporary Sociological Dilemma. 26 Sociological Q. 35 (1985).

Loffredo, Stephen. Poverty, Democracy and Constitutional Law. 141 U. Pa. L. Rev. 1277 (1993).

Lomasky, Loren E. Persons, Rights, and the Moral Community. 1987.

Loper v. New York City Police Dep't, 999 F.2d 699 (2d Cir. 1993).

Lovelace v. Gross, 537 N.Y.S.2d 783, 142 Misc. 2d 605 (Sup. 1989).

Lowenstein, Daniel H. The Failure of the Act: Conceptions of Law in *The Merchant of Venice, Bleak House, Les Miserables,* and Richard Weisberg's Poethics. 15 Cardozo L. Rev. 1139 (1994).

Lucas, J. R. Responsibility (1993).

Lujan v. Colorado State Bd. of Educ., 649 P.2d 1005 (Colo. 1982).

MacCallum, Gerald C., Jr. Negative and Positive Freedom. 76 Phil. Rev. 321 (1967).

MacGuigan, Mark R. St. Thomas and Legal Obligation. 35 New Scholasticism 281 (1961).

Machan, Tibor R. Human Rights and Human Liberties. 1975.

_____. Moral Myths and Basic Positive Rights. In Positive and Negative Duties. 33 Tulane Studies in Philosophy 35, ed. Eric Mack. 1985.

MacIntyre, Alasdair. How Moral Agents Became Ghosts, 53 Synthese 295 (1982).

Mackie, J. L. Obligations to Obey the Law. 67 Va. L. Rev. 143 (1981).

MacNeil, Ian R. The New Social Contract. 1980.

Margenau, Henry. The Laws of Nature Are Created by God. In Cosmos, Bios, Theos 57, ed. Henry Margenau and Roy A. Varghese. 1992.

Martin, Rex. A System of Rights. 1993.

Masters, Roger D. The Political Philosophy of Rousseau. 1968.

McConnell, Terrance C. Gratitude. 1993.

McCormick, Harvey L. Social Security Claims and Procedures. 4th ed., 1991.

McDonald, Forest. Novus Ordo Seclorum: The Intellectual Origins of the Constitution. 1985.

McFarland v. State, 784 S.W.2d 52 (Tex. Ct. Crim. App. 1990).

McGregor, Joan. Philips on Coerced Agreements. 7 Law and Phil. 225 (1988).

McIntyre, Alison. Compatibilists Could Have Done Otherwise: Responsibility and Negative Agency, 103 Phil. Rev. 453 (1993).

McPherson, Thomas. Political Obligation. 1967.

Melden, A. I. Rights and Persons. 1977.

Mellema, Gregory. On Being Fully Responsible. 21 Am. Phil. Q. 189 (1984).

Melnyk, Andrew. Is There a Formal Argument against Positive Rights? 55 Phil. Stud. 205 (1989).

Mercer, Mark Douglas. On a Pragmatic Argument against Pragmatism in Ethics. 30 Am. Phil. Q. 163 (1993).

Michelman, Frank I. In Pursuit of Constitutional Welfare Rights: One View of Rawls' Theory of Justice. 121 U. Pa. L. Rev. 962 (1973).

_____. Law's Republic. 97 Yale L. J. 1493 (1988).

_____. Welfare Rights in a Constitutional Democracy, 1979 Wash. U. L. Q. 659.

Mill, John Stuart. On Liberty, in On Liberty and Other Essays 5, ed. John Gray. 1991.

Miller, David. Social Justice. 1976.

Millich, Nancy A. Compassion Fatigue and the First Amendment: Are the Homeless Constitutional Castaways? 27 U.C. Davis L. Rev. 255 (1994).

Modagno, Louis. Comment, Brother, Can You Spare a Dime? The Panhandler's First Amendment Right to Beg, 5 Seton Hall Const. L. J. 681 (1995).

Moellendorf, Darrell. A Reconstruction of Hegel's Account of Freedom of the Will. 24 Owl of Minerva 5 (1992).

Montmarquet, James. Epistemic Virtue and Doxastic Responsibility. 29 Am. Phil. Q. 331 (1992).

Moore, Joan W. Isolation and Stigmatization in the Development of an Underclass: The Case of Chicano Gangs in East Los Angeles. 32 Social Probs. 1 (1985).

Moore, Michael S. Causation and the Excuses. 73 Cal. L. Rev. 1091 (1985).

_____. Choice, Character, and Excuse. 7 Social Phil. and Pol'y 29 (1990).

Moral Responsibility, ed. John Martin Fischer. 1986.

Morillo v. City of New York, 178 App. Div. 2d 7, 582 N.Y.S.2d 387 (1992).

Morse, Stephen J. Culpability and Control. 142 U. Pa. L. Rev. 1587 (1994).

_____. The Twilight of Welfare Criminology: A Final Word. 49 S. Cal. L. Rev. 1275 (1976).

_____. The Twilight of Welfare Criminology: A Reply to Judge Bazelon. 49 S. Cal. L. Rev. 1247 (1976).

Mulholland, Leslie A. Kant's System of Rights. 1990.

Mundle, C.W.K. Punishment and Desert, in Theories of Punishment 58, ed. Stanley E. Grupp. 1971.

Murdock v. Pennsylvania, 319 U.S. 105 (1943).

Murphy, Jeffrie G. Consent, Coercion, and Hard Choices. 67 Va. L. Rev. 79 (1981).

_____. Marxism and Retribution, 2 Phil. and Pub. Aff. 217 (1973).

Murphy, Mark C. Acceptance of Authority and the Duty to Comply with Just Institutions: A Comment on Waldron. 23 Phil. and Pub. Aff. 271 (1994).

Murphy, Nancey. Truth, Relativism, and Crossword Puzzles. 24 Zygon 299 (1989).

Narveson, Jan. Equality vs. Liberty: Advantage, Liberty. In Liberty and Equality 33, ed. Ellen Frankel Paul et al. 1985.

_____. Negative and Positive Rights. In Gewirth's Ethical Rationalism 96, ed. Edward Regis, Jr. 1984.

Nathan, Richard P. Will the Underclass Always Be with Us? 24 Society 57 (1987).

Natural Law Theory: Contemporary Essays, ed. Robert P. George. 1992.

Naylor, Margery B. Frankfurt on the Principle of Alternate Possibilities. 46 Phil. Stud. 249 (1984).

Neely, Wright. Freedom and Desire, 83 Phil. Rev. 32 (1974).

Neisser, Eric. Charging for Free Speech: User Fees and Insurance in the Marketplace of Ideas. 75 Geo. L. J. 257 (1985).

Neuman, Gerald L. Whose Constitution? 100 Yale L. J. 909 (1991).

Nickel, James W. Making Sense of Human Rights. 1987.

_____. Is There a Human Right to Employment? 10 Phil. F. 149 (1978).

Noonan, John T., Jr. Horses of the Night: Harris v. Vasquez. 45 Stan. L. Rev. 1011 (1993).

Nozick, Robert. Anarchy, State and Utopia. 1974.

_____. Philosophical Explanations. 1981.

_____. Coercion, in Philosophy, Science, and Method 440, ed. Sidney Morgenbesser et al. 1969.

Oakeshott, Michael. Hobbes on Civil Association. 1975.

Ogden v. Saunders, 25 U.S. (12 Wheat.) 213 (1827).

Olsen, Frances. The Family and the Market: A Study of Ideology and Legal Reform, 96 Harv. L. Rev. 1497 (1983).

O'Neill, Onora. Constructions of Reason: Explorations of Kant's Practical Philosophy. 1989.

_____. Rights, Obligations, and Needs. In Poverty, Justice, and the Law 29, ed. George R. Lucas, Jr. 1986.

_____. Book Review. 100 Mind 373 (1991).

Paine, Thomas. Rights of Man, ed. Philip S. Foner. 1974.

Paisner, Steven R. Comment, Compassion, Politics, and the Problem Lying on Our Sidewalks: A Legislative Approach for Cities to Address Homelessness. 67 Temple L. Rev. 1259 (1994).

Pateman, Carole. The Problem of Political Obligation. 2d ed., 1985.

Paton, H. J. The Categorical Imperative: A Study in Kant's Moral Philosophy. 1948.

Paulino v. Wright, 620 N.Y.S.2d 363 (App. Div. 1994), leave to appeal dismissed, 85 N.Y.2d 858, 648 N.E.2d 795, 624 N.Y.S.2d 375 (1995).

Paying for Jobs: Long-Term Unemployment. Economist, July 16, 1994, 48.

Peller, Gary. The Classical Theory of Law. 75 Cornell L. Rev. 300 (1988).

Penrose, Roger. The Emperor's New Mind. 1989.

Penry v. Lynaugh, 492 U.S. 302 (1989).

People v. Harris, 28 Cal. 3d 935, 623 P.2d 240, 171 Cal. Rptr. 679 (1981).

People v. Raszler, 169 Cal. App. 3d 1160, 215 Cal. Rptr. 770 (1985).

People v. Weber, 162 Cal. App. 3d Supp. 1, 208 Cal. Rptr. 719 (1984).

Pereira-Menault, Antonio Carlos. Against Positive Rights. 22 Val. U. L. Rev. 359 (1988).

Perry, Michael J. Taking Neither Rights-Talk Nor the "Critique of Rights" Too Seriously. 62 Tex. L. Rev. 1405 (1984).

Petersen, Carol D. Can JOBS Help the Underclass Break the Cycle of Poverty? 26 J. Econ. Issues 243 (1992).

Philips, Michael. Are Coerced Agreements Involuntary? 3 Law and Phil. 133 (1984).

Pico della Mirandola, Giovanni. Oration on the Dignity of Man, trans. A. Robert Caponigri. 1948.

Pildes, Richard H. Conceptions of Value in Legal Thought. 90 Mich. L. Rev. 1520 (1992).

Pillsbury, Samuel H. The Meaning of Deserved Punishment: An Essay on Choice, Character, and Responsibility. 67 Ind. L. J. 719 (1993).

Pitkin, Hanna. Obligation and Consent—I. 59 Am. Pol. Sci. Rev. 990 (1965).

Plamenatz, John. Consent, Freedom and Political Obligation. 2d ed., 1968.

_____. On le forcera d'etre libre. In Hobbes and Rousseau: A Collection of Critical Essays, ed. Maurice Cranston and Richard

Peters. 1972.

Plato. Euthyphro, Apology, Crito, and Phaedo, trans. Benjamin Jowett. 1988.

Poindexter, Georgette C. Towards a Legal Framework for Regional Redistribution of Poverty-Related Expenses. 47 Wash. U. J. Urban and Contemp. L. 3 (1995).

Political Ideas of St. Thomas Aquinas, The, ed. Dino Bigongiari. 1953) (Summa Theologica II-II, question 66, article 7).

Pottinger v. City of Miami, 40 F.3d 1155 (11th Cir. 1994) (remanding Pottinger v. City of Miami, 810 F. Supp. 1551 (S.D. Fla. 1992).

Pritchard, Michael S. Book Review. 45 Rev. Metaphysics 638 (1992).

Pritzker v. Merrill Lynch, Pierce, Fenner and Smith, Inc., 7 F.3d 1110 (3d Cir. 1993).

Raiffa, Howard. The Art and Science of Negotiation. 1982.

Rawls, John. Political Liberalism. 1993.

_____. A Theory of Justice. 1971.

Raz, Joseph. The Authority of Law. 1979.

_____. The Obligation to Obey: Revision and Tradition. 1 Notre Dame J. L., Ethics and Pub. Pol'y 139 (1984).

_____. On the Nature of Rights. 93 Mind 194 (1984).

Regan, Donald H. Law's Halo. 4 Social Phil. and Pol'y 15 (1986).

_____. Reasons, Authority, and the Meaning of "Obey": Further Thoughts on Raz and Obedience to Law. 3 Can. J. L. and Juris. 3 (1990).

Rescher, Nicholas. Welfare. 1972.

Respublica v. Chapman, 1 U.S. (1 Dall.) 53 (1781).

Ribton-Turner, C. J. A History of Vagrants and Vagrancy and Beggars and Begging. 1887. Patterson Smith ed., 1972.

Richards, David A. J. Foundations of American Constitutionalism. 1989.

Richards, Norvin. Acting Under Duress. 37 Phil. Q. 21 (1987).

_____. Luck and Desert. 95 Mind 198 (1986).

Ricketts, Erol R., and Isabel V. Sawhill. Defining and Measuring the Underclass. 7 J. Pol'y Analysis and Mgmt. 316 (1988).

Rifkin, Jeremy. The End of Work: The Decline of the Global Labor Force and the Dawn of the Post-Market Era. 1994.

Riley, Patrick. Locke On "Voluntary Agreement" and Political Power, 29 W. Pol. Q. 136 (1976).

Riordan, Thomas M. Note, Copping an Attitude: Rule of Law Lessons from the Rodney King Incident. 27 Loy. L.A. L. Rev. 675 (1994).

Ripstein, Arthur. Equality, Luck, and Responsibility. 23 Phil. and Pub. Aff. 3 (1994).

Roberts v. Louisiana, 431 U.S. 633, 646 (1977) (Rehnquist, J., dissenting).

Rodes, Robert E., Jr. The Legal Enterprise. 1976.

Roemer, John E. A Pragmatic Theory of Responsibility for the Egalitarian Planner. 22 Phil. and Pub. Aff. 146 (1993).

Rosenfeld, Michel. Contract and Justice: The Relation Between Classical Contract Law and Social Contract Theory. 70 Iowa L. Rev. 769 (1985).

Rothstein, Mark A. Employment Law. 1994.

Roulette v. City of Seattle, 850 F. Supp. 1442 (W.D. Wash. 1994).

Rousseau, Jean-Jacques. The Social Contract, trans. G.D.H. Cole. 1986.

Runciman, Walter Garrison. Relative Deprivation and Social Justice. Routledge ed., 1980.

Russell, Paul. Strawson's Way of Naturalizing Responsibility. 102 Ethics 287 (1992).

Russell, Robert J. The Meaning of Causality in Contemporary Physics. In Free Will and Determinism 13, ed. Viggo Mortensen and Robert C. Sorensen. 1987.

Sager, Lawrence Gene. Fair Measure: The Legal Status of Underenforced Constitutional Norms. 91 Harv. L. Rev. 1212 (1978).

Samura v. Kaiser Foundation Health Plan, Inc., 17 Cal. App. 4th 1284, 22 Cal. Rptr. 2d 20 (1993).

San Antonio Indep. School Dist. v. Rodriguez, 411 U.S. 1 (1973).

Sankowski, Edward. Two Forms of Moral Responsibility. 18 Phil. Topics 123 (1990).

Sartorius, Rolf. Political Authority and Political Obligation. 67 Va. L. Rev. 3 (1981).

Saunders, John T. The Temptations of "Powerlessness." 5 Am. Phil. Q. 100 (1968).

Sawhill, Isabel V. The Underclass: An Overview. 96 Pub. Interest 3 (1989).

_____. What about America's Underclass? 31 Challenge 27 (1988).

Scanlon, T. M. The Significance of Choice. In Equal Freedom 39, ed. Stephen Darwall. 1995.

Scheffler, Samuel. Responsibility, Reactive Attitudes, and Liberalism in Philosophy and Politics. 21 Phil. and Pub. Aff. 299 (1992).

Schelling, Thomas C. The Strategy of Conflict. 1960.

Scheppele, Kim Lane, and Jeremy Waldron. Contractarian Methods in Political and Legal Evaluation. 3 Yale J. L. and Humanities 195 (1991).

Schlossberger, Eugene. Moral Responsibility and Persons. 1992.

Schneider v. State, 308 U.S. 147 (1939).

Schwartz, Adina. Meaningful Work. 92 Ethics 634 (1982).

See, Katherine O'Sullivan. Comments from the Special Issues Editor: Approaching Poverty in the United States. 38 Social Probs. 427 (1991).

Seidler, Victor J. Kant, Respect, and Injustice: The Limits of Liberal Moral Theory. 1986.

Seneca, Lucius Annaeus. De Beneficiis. In 3 Moral Essays, trans. John W. Basore. William Heinemann Ltd. ed., 1958.

Serrano v. Priest, 18 Cal. 3d 728, 557 P.2d 929, 135 Cal. Rptr. 345 (1976).

Shanks, Niall. Quantum Mechanics and Determinism. 43 Phil. Q. 20 (1993).

Shaw v. Colonial Room, 175 Cal. App. 2d 845, 1 Cal. Rptr. 28 (1959).

Shevlin-Carpenter Co. v. Minnesota, 218 U.S. 57 (1910).

Shue, Henry. Basic Rights: Subsistence, Affluence, and U.S. Foreign Policy. 1980.

Simmons, A. John. Moral Principles and Political Obligations. 1979.

_____. Consent, Free Choice, and Democratic Government. 18 Ga. L. Rev. 791 (1984).

_____. The Principle of Fair Play. 8 Phil. and Pub. Aff. 307 (1979).

Simon, Harry. Towns Without Pity: A Constitutional and Historical Analysis of Official Efforts to Drive Homeless Persons from American Cities. 66 Tul. L. Rev. 631 (1992).

Simon, William H. Rights and Redistribution in the Welfare System. 38 Stan. L. Rev. 1431 (1986).

Singer, Beth J. Operative Rights. 1993.

Singleton v. State, 465 So. 2d 432 (Ala. Crim. App. 1983).

Sistare, C. T. Models of Responsibility in Criminal Theory: Comment on Baker. 7 Law and Phil. 295 (1989).

Slote, Michael. Book Review. 24 Int'l Stud. Phil. 138 (1992).

_____. Ethics without Free Will. 16 Soc. Theory and Prac. 369 (1990).

Smiley, Marion. Responsibility and the Boundaries of Community. 1993.

Smith, David M. Note, A Theoretical and Legal Challenge to Homeless Criminalization as Public Policy. 12 Yale L. and Pub. Pol'y Rev. 487 (1994).

Smith, Holly. Culpable Ignorance. 92 Phil. Rev. 543 (1983).

Smith, M. B. E. Is There a Prima Facie Obligation to Obey the Law? 83 Yale L. J. 950 (1973).

Snyder v. United States, 461 U.S. 907 (1983).

Southwark London Borough Council v. Williams, 1971 L.R.—Ch. 734 (Ch. App. 1971).

Spector, Horacio. Autonomy and Rights: The Moral Foundations of Liberalism. 1992.

Stanford v. Kentucky, 492 U.S. 361 (1989) (Brennan, J., dissenting).

State v. Burkemper, 882 S.W.2d 193 (Mo. Ct. App. 1994).

State v. Chisholm, 882 P.2d 974 (Idaho Ct. App. 1994).

State v. Gann, 244 N.W.2d 746 (N. Dak. 1976).

State v. Greer, 879 S.W.2d 683 (Mo. Ct. App. 1994).

State v. Kopsa, 887 P.2d 57 (Idaho Ct. App. 1994).

State v. Moe, 174 Wash. 303, 24 P.2d 638 (1933).

Steiner, Hillel. An Essay on Rights. 1994.

Steward Machine Co. v. Davis, 301 U.S. 548 (1937).

Strawson, Galen. Freedom and Belief. 1986.

_____. Consciousness, Free Will, and the Unimportance of Determinism. 32 Inquiry 3 (1989).

_____. The Impossibility of Moral Responsibility. 75 Phil. Stud. 5 (1994).

Strawson, Peter F. Freedom and Resentment. In Free Will 59, ed. Gary Watson. 1982.

Stump, Eleonore. Sanctification, Hardening of the Heart, and Frankfurt's Concept of Free Will. 85 J. Phil. 395 (1988).

Sullivan, Roger J. Immanuel Kant's Moral Theory. 1989.

Sumner, L. W. The Moral Foundation of Rights. 1987.

Sunstein, Cass R. The Partial Constitution. 1993.

_____. Beyond the Republican Revival. 97 Yale L. J. 1539 (1988).

Swinburne, Richard. Responsibility and Atonement. 1989.

Symposium. 44 Mercer L. Rev. 521-77 (1993) (contributions by Professors Chemerinsky, Gedicks, Dorin, and Ferrara).

Symposium, 1979 Wash. U. L.Q. 659-733 (articles and commentary by Professors Michelman, Bork, Levin, and Appleton).

Symposium: Homelessness and the Law. 23 Stetson L. Rev. 327 (1994).

Symposium: Positive and Negative Duties. Tulane Studies in Philosophy no. 33, ed. Eric Mack 1985.

Szasz, Thomas S. Law, Liberty and Psychiatry: An Inquiry into the Social Uses of Mental Health Practices. 1963.

Taylor, Charles. Human Agency and Language. 1985.

_____. What's Wrong with Negative Liberty? 2 Philosophy and the Human Sciences 211 (1985).

Tennessee v. Garner, 471 U.S. 1 (1985).

Thomas Aquinas, Saint. On Law, Morality, and Politics, ed. William P. Baumgarth and Richard J. Regan. (Summa Theologica II-II, question 66, article 7).

_____. Summa Theologica I-II, questions 91-97.

Thompson v. Oklahoma, 487 U.S. 815 (1988).

Thomson, Judith Jarvis. The Realm of Rights. 1990.

_____. Rights, Restitution, and Risk: Essays in Moral Theory, ed. William Parent. 1986.

Thurlow v. Massachusetts, 46 U.S. (5 How.) 504, 632 (1847) (Grier, J., concurring).

Timmer, Doug A. et al. Paths to Homelessness: Extreme Poverty and the Urban Housing Crisis. 1994.

Tobe v. City of Santa Ana, 27 Cal. App. 4th 1209, 27 Cal. Rptr. 2d 386 (1994), rev'd, 9 Cal. 4th 1069, 892 P.2d 1145, 40 Cal. Rptr. 2d 402 (1995).

Trebilcock, Michael. The Limits of Freedom of Contract. 1993.

Tucker v. Toia, 43 N.Y.2d 1, 371 N.E.2d 449, 400 N.Y.S.2d 728 (1977).

Tushnet, Mark. An Essay on Rights. 62 Tex. L. Rev. 1363 (1984).

Tussman, Joseph. Obligation and the Body Politic. 1960.

The Underclass: Hearing Before the Joint Economic Comm., 101st Cong., 1st sess. 1989.

United States Code title 28 § 994 (d) (1995).

United States v. Bailey, 444 U.S. 394 (1980).

United States v. Bevans, 16 U.S. (3 Wheat.) 336 (1818).

United States v. Carter, 436 F.2d 200 (D.C. Cir. 1970) (Bazelon, C.J., concurring).

United States v. Kras, 409 U.S. 434 (1973).

United States v. Manzella, 719 F.2d 1263 (7th Cir. 1986).

United States v. Moore, 486 F.2d 1139 (D.C. Cir.) (Wright, J., dissenting), cert. denied, 414 U.S. 980 (1973).

United States v. Scott, 437 U.S. 82 (1978).

United States v. Verdugo-Urquidez, 856 F.2d 1214, 1231-32 (9th Cir. 1988) (Wallace, J., dissenting), rev'd on other grounds, 494 U.S. 259 (1990).

Vanhorne's Lessee v. Dorrance, 2 U.S. (2 Dall.) 304 (1795).

Van Inwagen, Peter. Ability and Responsibility, in Moral Responsibility 153, ed. John Martin Fischer. 1986.

_____. Response to Slote. 16 Soc. Theory and Prac. 385 (1990).

Vihelin, Kadri. Stop Me before I Kill Again. 75 Phil. Stud. 115 (1994).

Vogel, Lawrence. Understanding and Blaming: Problems in the Attribution of Moral Responsibility. 53 Phil. and Phenomenological Res. 129 (1993).

Vuoso, George. Background, Responsibility, and Excuse. 96 Yale L. J. 1661 (1987).

Waldron, Jeremy. Liberal Rights. 1993.

_____. Homelessness and the Issue of Freedom. 39 UCLA L. Rev. 295 (1991).

Walker, A. D. M. Political Obligation and the Argument from Gratitude. 17 Phil. and Pub. Aff. 191 (1988).

Walker v. Rowe, 791 F.2d 507 (7th Cir.), cert. denied, 479 U.S. 994 (1986).

Wallace, R. Jay. Responsibility and the Moral Sentiments. 1994.

Waller, Bruce N. Freedom Without Responsibility. 1990.

_____. Denying Moral Responsibility: The Difference It Makes. 49 Analysis 44 (1989).

_____. Determinism and the Principle of Vacuous Contrast. 19 Metaphilosophy 65 (1988).

_____. Freedom Without Responsibility. 20 Behavior and Phil. 71 (1992).

_____. Natural Autonomy and Alternative Possibilities. 30 Am. Phil. Q. 73 (1993).

_____. A Response to Kane and Hocutt. 20 Behavior and Phil. 83 (1992).

_____. Responsibility and the Self-Made Self. 53 Analysis 45 (1993).

Walsh, Adrian J. Meaningful Work as a Distributive Good. 32 S. J. Phil. 233 (1994).

Walzer, Michael. Spheres of Justice. 1983.

Ward, Andrew. On Kant's Defence of Moral Freedom, 8 Hist. Phil. Q. 373 (1991).

Warr, Peter, Paul Jackson, and Michael Banks. Unemployment and Mental Health: Some British Studies. 44 J. Social Issues 47 (1988).

Warrender, Howard. The Political Philosophy of Hobbes. 1957.

Washington v. Davis, 426 U.S. 229 (1976).

Watson, Gary. Responsibility and the Limits of Evil: Variations on a Strawsonian Theme. In Responsibility, Character, and the Emotions 256, ed. Ferdinand Schoeman. 1987.

_____. Free Action and Free Will. 96 Mind 145 (1987).

Weinreb, Lloyd L. Natural Law and Justice. 1987.

_____. Desert, Punishment, and Criminal Responsibility. 49 Law and Contemp. Probs. 47 (1986).

Weiss, Roslyn. The Moral and Social Dimensions of Gratitude. 23 S. J. Phil. 491 (1985).

Weithman, Paul J. Waldron on Political Legitimacy and the Social Minimum. 45 Phil. Q. 218 (1995).

Wellman, Carl. Welfare Rights. 1982.

Wertheimer, Alan. Coercion. 1986.

West, Cornel. Race Matters. 1993.

Westlye v. Look Sports, Inc., 17 Cal. App. 4th 1715, 22 Cal. Rptr. 2d 781 (1993).

White, Alan R. Rights. 1984.

White, Morton. Philosophy, The Federalist, and the Constitution. 1987.

Widerker, David, and Charlotte Katzoff. Book Review. 90 J. Phil. 98 (1993).

_____. Book Review. 54 Analysis 285 (1994).

Wiggins, David. Towards a Reasonable Libertarianism. In Essays on Freedom of Action 31, ed. Ted Honderich. 1973.

Wilkinson v. Leland, 27 U.S. (2 Pet.) 627, 657 (1829) (Story, J., for the Court).

Williams, Bernard. Shame and Necessity. 1993.

_____. Voluntary Acts and Responsible Agents. 10 Oxford J. Legal Stud. 1 (1990).

Williams, Glanville. The Theory of Excuses. 1982 Crim. L. Rev. 732.

Wilson, William Julius. The Truly Disadvantaged (1987).

_____. American Social Policy and the Ghetto Underclass. 35 Dissent 57 (1988).

_____. Studying Inner-City Dislocations: The Challenge of Public Agenda Research, 56 Am. Sociological Rev. 1 (1991).

Winter, Ralph K., Jr. Poverty, Economic Equality, and the Equal Protection Clause. 1972 S. Ct. Rev. 41 (P. Kurland ed., 1973).

Wolch, Jennifer and Michael Dear. Malign Neglect: Homelessness in an American City. 1993.

Wolf, Susan. Freedom Within Reason. 1990.

_____. The Importance of Free Will. 90 Mind 386 (1981).

Wolff, Jonathan. Political Obligation, Fairness, and Independence. 8 Ratio 87 (1995).

Wolff, Robert Paul. The Autonomy of Reason. 1973.

_____. In Defense of Anarchism. 1970.

Wood, Gordon S. The Creation of the American Republic 1776-1787. 1969.

Wright, J. Skelly. Politics and the Constitution: Is Money Speech? 85 Yale L. J. 1001 (1976).

Wright, R. George. Reason and Obligation. 1994.

_____. Could a Constitutional Amendment Be Unconstitutional? 22 Loyola U. Chi. L. Rev. 741 (1991).

_____. Should the Law Reflect the World? Lessons for Legal Theory from Quantum Mechanics. 18 Fla. St. U. L. Rev. 855 (1991).

Yellen, David, and Deborah Young. Federal Sentencing Law and Practice. 2d ed., 1994.

Zimmerman, David. Coercive Wage Offers. 10 Phil. and Pub. Aff. 121 (1981).

_____. Moral Responsibility, Freedom, and Alternate Possibilities. 63 Pac. Phil. Q. 243 (1982).

Zimmerman, Michael J. Luck and Moral Responsibility, 97 Ethics 374 (1987).

Zola, Emile. Work, trans. Ernest A. Vizetelly. 1925.

Zupanec, Donald M. Annotation, Coercion, Compulsion, or Duress as Defense to Charge of Robbery, Larceny, or Related Crime. 1 A. L. R. 4th 481 (1980).

index